Surviving PTSD, The Invisible War A Combat Marine's Story

By
Rodney R. Letchworth
LtCol USMC Retired

Dedicated To

Dr. Aida Saldivia, Md.

Atlanta Veterans Administration Hospital

Who kept me alive for 8 years with Monthly ECT TREATMENTS

And To

D. Keith Ivey, MSW

Mental Health Counselor

Who taught me how to live with PTSD

And To

All Family Members of Combat Vets who have watched with despair as their Loved Ones have fought an Invisible War, and slowly descended into that PTSD pit!

Copyright @ 2014 by Rodney Letchworth
All Rights Reserved

ISBN-13: 978-1502753045

Surviving PTSD   A Combat Marine's Story

Table of Contents   Page

Chapter One – Memories of War   4

Chapter Two - Eyewitness to Murder   14

Chapter Three – Leak in the U.S. Attorney's Office   25

Chapter Four – First Flight to Florida   30

Chapter Five – The Trial   45

Chapter Six - Return to Atlanta   52

Chapter Seven – Second Flight to Florida   63

Chapter Eight – Mafia Hit Contract   70

Chapter Nine – Hiding in Coral Gables   105

Chapter Ten – Flashbacks to Combat   112

Chapter Eleven – Return to Florida, New Life   132

Chapter Twelve – Wakulla Volcano   136

Chapter Thirteen – Move to NC. Mountains   160

Chapter Fourteen – Leave Mountains, back to Florida 173

Chapter Fifteen – ECT Failure, Suicide Attempt   177

Chapter Sixteen – Suicide Attempt Failure   180

Chapter Seventeen – Living with PTSD   183

Epilogue   192

Recourses   194

Chapter One

Memories of War in Vietnam

Beginning of the Tet Offensive

The Battle of Hue

It was January 29, 1968. I had been ordered by my Air Group Commander to go to the old Imperial City, Hue and confer with the U.S. Air Force Forward Air Controllers (FAC's). These FAC's were based at a small air strip inside the walls and moat of the ancient medieval city of Hue.

My commander wanted to improve communications between our two organizations. Our pilots worked together with their pilots providing close air support to Army and Marine Corps combat units. My commander felt that establishing a personal relationship with the FACS could be beneficial, and had therefore set up this meeting.

Hue is a city more than 1000 years old. It is surrounded by a medieval wall and a moat. Inside the Walls are a citadel, legislative buildings, a huge university campus, many homes and businesses; and the small Air Force airstrip. The city also had a massive civilian population.

I caught a transport flight from my base at Chu Lai, South Vietnam, to Da Nang, South Vietnam, and spent the night. The next morning, Jan 29, 1968, I caught a ride to Hue in the back seat of one of the Forward Air Controller's small observation aircraft. This was his daily mail flight between Da Nang and Hue.

I spent a very pleasant day getting acquainted with the pilots I had only known by their "call sign". They were delighted to meet an A4 Skyhawk pilot. We compared notes about every aspect of our teamwork, and they were very complimentary about our skill in the A4 in being able to put our bombs on target with great accuracy.

They were less than complimentary about some of the fighter pilots who had been put into service dropping bombs. This was understandable. Fighter pilots were accustomed to flying around at 35,000 ft. trying to shoot down enemy planes – not flying around at 50 ft. dropping bombs.

That evening the FAC's invited me to join them at their homemade bar down in the basement of their headquarters which was the MACV compound, previously a large hotel.

About midnight, two Australian Army officers walked into the bar. They had been out to check up on one of their Regiments up near the DMZ- (North Vietnamese Border). These two looked as if someone had dragged them through the dirt all day. Their uniforms were covered with dirt. They said "Come outside! We'll show you something you won't believe!"

We followed them outside, and there was an ordinary jeep. All that was different about this jeep, though, was that there was not one square foot of metal on the vehicle which did not have a bullet hole in it!

Then they told us what had happened. They said, "We were driving back from visiting our men up north, when a rifle round hit the windshield and passed between us. Without any hesitation we both rolled out our side of the jeep and into the ditch. The Jeep kept going. We knew we were goners as we watched that jeep going down the road being riddled with hundreds of bullets.

When the jeep came to a curve in the road, it didn't make the curve. It hit the ditch and rolled over. The motor stopped running and everything got really quiet.

We knew we would be next as we waited and waited, but nothing happened. After two hours of absolute quiet, it got dark and we got up and walked to the jeep. We turned it back up on its wheels. We got in, cranked it up and drove it home." "This is a real mystery! We have no idea what's is going on!"

None of us could offer any ideas of our own. What in the world might have caused this to happen? None of us could offer any explanation.

After another round of drinks, we all retired to our rooms to get some sleep. No telling what would happen next!

Next morning, January, 30th, well before daylight, I caught a ride in the back seat of the mail flight, going back to Da Nang. We took off just before dawn on the runway heading east.

The Sun was below the horizon and when we got high enough to see over the wall around the old city, I beheld one of the most beautiful sights I have ever seen in this world.

There before me was the South China Sea before sunrise. There was not a cloud in the sky. But every imaginable color was there, right in front of me. I'll never forget that picture as long as I live.

At Da Nang I caught a ride in a transport back to Chu Lai. When I stepped off the plane, at Chu Lai, a Corporal from my squadron came running up.

"Captain, Captain, come quick!" he said. "They've overrun Hue! We're launching everything! Hurry, Hurry!"

I raced to the ready room, changed into my flight suit, launched with my wingman, flew to Hue and dropped bombs on the city I had left only a few hours before!

As I was making a bombing run on a machine gun emplacement on top of the wall, beside the moat, something caught my eye off to the right. I glanced over and there floating in the moat, tail up, cockpit submerged, was the mail flight aircraft, the birddog, I had ridden to Da Nang in only a few hours before. <u>There were no survivors!</u>

The Battle of Khe Sanh

At Khe Sanh, my wingman was hit by ground fire and had to punch out (eject). I spotted his parachute and made passes by him, shooting every 3rd or 4th pass to keep the NVA troops away from him until one of our helicopters could come in and pick him up.

As the Army helo was hovering over him, lowering a rope for him to grab, it came under heavy ground fire and had to leave. My wingman had already grabbed the rope and had wrapped it around his chest, but had no time to tie it. So he just held the rope and the end which he had wrapped around his chest together as the helo lifted off.

I held my breath until the helo and my wingman got clear of the area and over friendly territory. The helo then lowered him to the ground. After he was safely on the ground, the helo landed and let him climb aboard for the trip home.

I later found out from my wingman that the crew chief, who had lowered the rope to him, was also caught by surprise when they began getting heavy ground fire. The crew chief did not have time to tie his end of the rope either. He just hurriedly wrapped the rope around his right arm, and grasped the two ends of the rope in his right hand. He then quickly thrust his left arm up to the elbow through the webbing of the seat back of the 'jump seat' at the door of the helo. He was determined not to leave my wingman on the ground in the middle of that nest of murdering beasts.

As the helo lifted off, the Crew Chief had been jerked outside the helo. He was dangling outside of the helo, holding my wingman's rope in his right hand and with his left arm hooked thru the webbing of the jump seat! He was so determined to save my wingman; he just hung on until the helo reached a safe place to land and load my wingman inside the helo.

That man was a real HERO in my book. I wrote a letter to his Commanding Officer recommending him for a Silver Star Medal. I later learned that the man had been awarded the Silver Star Medal on my recommendation.

What a proud moment that was for me!

The Battle of the A Shau Valley

The A Shau Valley is a valley running North and South just west of the Marine Airbase at Khe Sanh. The valley is better known by its nickname – "The Ho Chi Min Trail".

The Marine Corps operated an airbase, (Khe Sanh) on top of a mountain at the southern end of "The Trail". Four observation posts, two on Hill 881 and two on Hill 861 overlooking the A Shau Valley north of the airbase, were manned continuously by Marine Corps troops. This was done in order to observe activity on the "The Trail", i.e. Communist troops moving south out of North Vietnam.

Between the base and the outposts was some very rugged terrain. This area was controlled by the NVA – North Vietnamese Army.

The outposts had to be resupplied by Helicopters. One of our missions was to "escort" the Helo's on each of their resupply missions. We operated in pairs of two A4's, one on each side of the helo's flight path firing our 20 MM guns into the jungle canopy in order to keep the NVA from firing on our helo's.

When the "Tet Offensive" occurred, 20,000 NVA fighters emerged from their hiding places around the

Marine Corp airbase and assaulted the base. The assault lasted for weeks.

On one mission, I was assigned a machine gun emplacement not more than 30 feet from the runway pavement and 100 yards from the approach end of the runway. I scored a direct hit on the little (expletive deleted)! No transports had been able to land or take off for several days. This went on for weeks as the base was under attack until it was finally evacuated. One of my friends from the Blacksheep Squadron of years before had transitioned into flying the C-130 Transports. I found out later that he was killed during this battle when a mortar round landed in his cockpit while he was parked on the ramp loading troops during the evacuation.

Ten years after returning from Combat in Vietnam, I retired as a Lieutenant Colonel and moved my family to Atlanta, Ga. where I began a new career as a Stock Broker with Dean Whitter.

Chapter Two

Eyewitness to Murder

October 25th 1978, dawned as a beautiful balmy Atlanta morning. After an uneventful morning at work, I was driving along Riverside Road on my way home for lunch. The road ambled along the south side of the Chattahoochee River passing through a semirural wooded area. There were large Estate Homes on the right side of the road, and undeveloped river front lots on the left side. As I topped a small rise in the road I saw a car parked off the pavement on the left side of the road, facing me. The car was a beautiful, powder blue Mercedes Sports Coupe. A young, blonde woman was seated behind the wheel, and a young man was lifting a rifle out of the open trunk of the car.

At that moment, my attention was diverted by a movement to my left. I turned and saw a middle-aged man holding a shotgun in his left hand. He was standing by a wooden gate going into a large vacant riverside lot. He had what appeared to be a black, curly haired wig on his head. It was totally out of character with the rest of his attire. Also memorable was a huge, open mouth grin! I assumed the two men were going into the woods to shoot ducks or some other type of game along the river. In 15 seconds or so I was past the scene.

I had a pleasant lunch with my wife and returned to work along the same route. The blue Mercedes and the three people were gone, and there was nothing unusual as I passed the site.

That evening after work as I approached the location I was stopped by a line of traffic several hundred feet long. A police officer was stopping each car and asking questions. When it was my turn, the officer asked, "Sir were you along this road earlier today?" "Why yes", I replied; "I came home for lunch about 12 o'clock and passed again going back to work about an hour later." "Did you see anything unusual", he asked? "Not really, I answered, there were just two men going into the woods with guns. I assumed they were going hunting."

"Pull over!" the officer ordered.

After I pulled over, a plain clothed officer approached and began asking questions. "What did you see when you passed here this morning?" He asked. I replied, "There were two men going into the woods. Each of them had a gun, and a young lady was sitting in a blue Mercedes Sports Coupe. I assumed the men were going hunting."

He asked, "Can you describe them?" "Yes sir", I said. "There was a middle-aged man, about 45 to 50 years old, standing by that gate over there. He had a shotgun in his left hand. He appeared to be of Mediterranean descent. His hair was black but it looked like a curly wig that really didn't fit him. He also had the biggest grin on his face you've ever seen. The other man was younger and he was lifting a rifle out of the trunk of the car. The woman was blonde and very attractive. She was seated in the driver's seat of the car. The car was a flashy, powder blue Mercedes Sports Coupe."

The officer recorded my name, address, phone number and gave me his business card. The card read, "Paul King, FBI Agent." "Call me if you remember anything else!" he said. "Yes sir", I replied, and then I drove away toward home.

The next morning, as I walked into my boss's office, I glanced down at the morning Atlanta Journal-Constitution newspaper on his conference table. There on the front page was a large photo of the man I had seen the day before. The one standing at the gate holding the shotgun in his left hand. The caption under the photo read: "Fugitive Mob Boss's Lieutenant Murdered, Mob Boss Suspected". I sat down and picked up the paper. This was all new information for me. I had only been in Atlanta a few months and was not acquainted with the story of Michael Thevis, Mob Boss, and now an out of control, wanted criminal.

Yesterday, the newspaper story continued, Roger Underhill, a former Mob Member and criminal associate of Michael Thevis, had been killed in a wooded area off Riverside Drive in Atlanta.

I left my boss's office and returned to mine. In my billfold I found the card which had been given to me by the plain clothed officer at the traffic stop the day before. With trembling hands I dialed the number for "Paul King, FBI Agent." When he answered, I told him who I was and then literally exploded. "The man I saw yesterday standing at the gate with a gun in his hand - his picture is on the front page of this morning's paper!"

Paul King calmly replied, "Yes sir, we know, but you don't need to be worried about it. We won't need you as a witness. We have many of his friends helping us. We won't need your help at all. Just forget about it". Relief flooded my whole body. Wow! What a close call! Back to work, I went.

I did, however, keep up with the stories in the daily paper over the next several weeks. Michael Thevis had started as a youngster working in the pornography business after dropping out of Georgia Tech. He turned out to be a very good crook and after a few years had progressed to the point where he had attracted the attention of the New York Mafia. The Mafia eventually installed him as the boss of their operations in the five southeastern states. Thevis became a very, very, wealthy individual.

After many years, however, he had experienced several run-ins with law enforcement. He eventually became an embarrassment to the mob. The mob bosses decided to replace him as head of their operations. At about the same time federal law enforcement officers had begun to arrest many of his henchmen in an effort to make a case against him under the RICO (Racketeering Influenced Corrupt Organizations) Act.

One of Thevis' chief lieutenants, Roger Underhill, had been arrested and charged with a number of crimes. Roger was confined in the federal prison in Atlanta and had been offered many benefits, including the Federal Witness Protection Program, if he would agree to testify against his boss, Michael Thevis. Underhill steadfastly refused to cooperate. Thevis however, wasn't sure Underhill would remain loyal, so he put out a contract to have Roger killed right there in the US Federal Prison in

Atlanta. The hit was attempted by another inmate inside the prison.

The hit was unsuccessful! After Underhill survived the attempted assassination he realized that he would never be safe from Michael Thevis. So he offered to tell all he knew in exchange for a new life in the Federal Witness Protection Program. After Roger was accepted into the Witness Protection Program, he proceeded to tell all he knew.

More than 40 hours of videotaped testimony were recorded in which Roger told all about the 20 years of murder, intimidation, graft and corruption he had witnessed and participated in while he was an accomplice of Michael Thevis.

Part of the Witness Protection Program acceptance process is to have the witness dispose of all his tangible personal property, investments, and anything else which could be traced by the Mob. The Mob would most certainly be determined to find and kill him.

Roger owned a large wooded lot on the Chattahoochee River off River Road which needed to be sold. He listed the property with a Realtor who found a prospective buyer. Roger was released from the Federal Prison for one day with permission to show the property to the prospective buyer. The information about this appointment time and place was purchased by Michael Thevis through his Mob connections.

When Roger and his prospective buyer, Isaac Galanti, a prominent Atlanta Businessman, showed up at the site, Michael Thevis and his accomplice were waiting with guns ready. Both Roger Underhill and Atlanta businessman Isaac Galanti were brutally murdered.

Two weeks after the murders Michael Thevis, his girlfriend Jeanette Evans, and her cousin, Bart Hood, were arrested in Massachusetts. They were riding in a powder blue Mercedes Sports Coupe. Inside the trunk of the car the police found a rifle, a shotgun, $600,000 in cash; and $1 Million Dollars in diamonds. They were headed out of the country. Descriptions of all three people and the automobile exactly matched the descriptions I had given to the FBI at the traffic stop. I was extremely happy that I would not be needed as a witness at <u>that</u> trial! It would certainly not have been conducive to my longevity!

My job was that of a Stockbroker. I had been in the business less than a year. I'd started working as a Stockbroker in California where I was stationed during my last year in the US Marine Corps. I had retired in November, 1977, and worked there in California as a Stockbroker until June 1978. When my kids finished their school year we moved to Atlanta. I bought a home near the entrance to the Atlanta Country Club, and reported to the Dean Witter brokerage office in Phipps Plaza, about four miles from our new home.

Stockbrokers are generally not paid a salary. We earned our money from commission sales. When starting a new career as a stockbroker however, the standard procedure is to be paid an advance on future commissions until enough commissions have been accumulated to repay the advances. Then we are strictly on our own, nothing but commissions. The only income we received was a percentage of the commissions we generated for our firm.

A new stockbroker moving into a new city must find his own clients and recommend financial transactions such as purchasing or selling stocks or bonds which generate commissions for the firm. To be successful as a stockbroker one must work very hard to find new clients; study the market to find appropriate investment opportunities; and then persuade the new clients to take advantage of these opportunities. Individuals who are successful in finding new clients and persuading them to invest in opportunities which actually become successful are in great demand in the securities industry. I had been successful in California finding new investors and making profitable investments on their behalf and therefore I had no difficulty finding a new job in Atlanta. Now that the initial scare of becoming involved in a murder trial with very high visibility had passed, I put my mind to work finding new investors, studying the market, finding new investment opportunities and staying busy.

Time passed very fast for me and I was very happy for about six months. Then one day I received a call from the manager of the largest Merrill Lynch brokerage office in Atlanta. He asked to have lunch with me. At lunch he made me an offer I could not refuse. The offer included a substantial increase in pay which included a large salary for six months followed by a large percentage of commissions earned for another year after that. I accepted his offer and left Dean Witter.

I went to work for Merrill Lynch, moving to the First National Bank Building, fifth floor, downtown Atlanta. Life was wonderful! I was making more money than I had ever made in my life!

All that was about to change!

Chapter Three

Security Leak in the Atlanta U. S. Attorney's Office

One day a stranger knocked on my office door and asked to speak to me. I thought he wanted to talk about investments so I invited him in. He introduced himself and told me he was a Private Investigator working for Defense Attorney Bobby Lee Cook who was representing Michael Thevis.

He said, "We understand you are going to be a witness in this trial, and we want to know what you are going to testify about."

WOW! What a shock! I almost swallowed my teeth! Trying to maintain my composure, I said "Just a moment. Before we start, I have to go see my boss for a second. I'll be right back."

I went to a vacant office around the corner, and down the hall. I checked to see if he had followed me. He hadn't, so I closed the door and sat down. I then dialed the U. S. Attorney, Craig Gillen. I had been keeping up with the news and knew he would be the Prosecuting Attorney at the trial.

When he came on the line, I introduced myself and then proceeded to tell him that FBI agent Paul King had assured me I would not be called as a witness. But now I have a man in my office who works for Bobby Lee Cook, the Defense Attorney for Michael Thevis. He wants to know what I will say when I get on the witness stand.

The Assistant U.S. Attorney for the Northern District of Georgia let out a yell. "My God! I've got a leak in my organization!" "Nobody knows you are going to be a witness – not even you!" Then he became very quiet.

After a few moments he said; "Mr. Letchworth, you are in grave danger. Your wife and children are also in grave danger. I don't know where to tell you to go for help! Obviously, I can't trust anyone in my office anymore".

"Please don't <u>even call here again</u> asking for help. Take your family and get out of town. Hide somewhere where no one can find you or any member of your family. Don't talk to anyone but the FBI. I <u>think</u> it will be safe for you to talk to the F.B.I. but I don't know!"

He paused and then said, "I'll need you at the Trial. Call the F.B.I. when you safely can. Leave them a phone number where you can be reached. I'll need you at the trial. The F.B.I. will call and tell you when to come to Rome, Georgia where the trial is being held. When you get to Rome don't talk to anyone except the F.B.I. They will tell you how to find them and they will protect you while you are there.

After this is all over, if things get really bad, <u>I can always get you into the Witness Protection Program.</u> Be careful and good luck!"

I hung up the phone and without any hesitation, left the borrowed office, went down a back stairway to the basement where my car was parked. I got into my car and raced away. I said nothing to my boss or to anyone else; I just got in the car and drove away.

My wife had recently opened a new business – a ladies exercise salon. I drove directly to her salon, went inside and told her we had to leave town immediately! The mob was looking for me. I told her not to say anything to anyone about why she was closing her shop or where we were going.

I then explained that we had to get the children out of their schools, pack our bags, and leave town immediately. I told her it was not safe for any of us to stay in Atlanta. I told her I would go to the high school and get our two girls out of their classes and meet her at home as soon as she could go to the elementary school and get our two boys out of their classes.

We all arrived at home about the same time. I explained to the family that something <u>terrible</u> had just happened and it was no longer safe for any of us to stay in Atlanta. I told everyone to go inside and pack a suitcase with as many clothes as they could find room for and load both automobiles as quickly as we could. I collected all the guns and ammo I had in the house and loaded them into my car. In about an hour we were packed and ready to go.

Without saying goodbye to anyone we got into our two cars and drove away. We had no idea where we would end up, or when we could return. My boss could not be notified that I would be leaving or when I would get back. My wife's customers could not be notified that her salon would be closed or when they could expect to return and continue using the salon for which they had paid in advance their monthly fees. Our children's teachers could not be advised of our status or when the children would return to school. Even our families could not be notified of our whereabouts. It would be dangerous to use credit cards, so we went by our bank and withdrew all of the cash in all of our bank accounts. We just disappeared off the face of the earth!

Chapter Four

First Flight to Florida

Not knowing if we were being followed, I led our small caravan onto Interstate 20 going west out of Atlanta toward Birmingham. Then it was time to put to use some of my Marine Corps training in the art of escape and evasion. I was constantly on extreme alert, watching each car in front of me and behind me for any unusual activity.

I varied speed; constantly speeding up and watching the traffic to see if any other vehicle was changing speed at the same time. Then I slowed down to the minimum speed for the interstate highway. I maintained that speed until all the traffic around me disappeared in the distance ahead.

After crossing into Alabama I took the first exit off the interstate. I stopped on the off ramp and watched my rearview mirror to see if any of the vehicles on the interstate had slowed or followed me off the interstate. We remained parked on the ramp for more than an hour watching for any unusual activity.

When I was satisfied that we were not being followed, I circled from the off ramp to the on ramp and proceeded back on the interstate toward Atlanta. After crossing from Alabama into Georgia I exited the interstate and proceeded south. We took <u>only</u> secondary roads from there to Florida, constantly taking detours on country roads to the east and to the west.

I was always on alert for any suspicious automobiles which might be following us. My destination was my brother's farm, located between Tallahassee, Florida, and Monticello, Florida. Of course, my brother had no idea we were coming, but I knew he was the best one to give me advice on how to handle this very delicate and dangerous situation.

Larry's farm was in a very remote area with a single lane unpaved road about a mile long running from the nearest paved highway to his property. Larry and his wife Rosa had purchased the property because: in the center of the property was the tallest Indian Mound east of the Mississippi River.

After purchasing the property, Larry and Rosa built a lovely three-bedroom brick home right beside the Indian mound.

Larry was a federal law enforcement officer working at the Federal Correctional Institution (FCI) in Tallahassee. I knew he could help us find a solution to this very delicate and dangerous problem, if anyone could.

We arrived unannounced at Larry and Rosa's farm about midnight. They graciously invited us in. I explained our dilemma to Larry and asked for his advice and help.

"Well", he said, "the first thing to do is to get the family inside the house and get the children bedded down".

I tried to discuss looking for some other safe place for us to hide the family until this crisis was over.

Larry and Rosa would not listen to anything except that our entire family stays with them for the duration of the crisis.

Their home was a beautiful three bedroom brick home which was perfect for their family which included two children, Beth and Robert. However, it was extremely crowded after we moved two additional adults and four additional children into the home.

I will never cease to be grateful for the wonderful hospitality their family provided our family. This hospitality continued for a much longer period of time than any of us could have imagined.

The first thing we did was to hide our two automobiles in the woods near the Indian mound and disguise them with small limbs. The automobiles never left that location for the next 30 days. Next morning we began to organize our families into shifts so that some could be off duty, getting some sleep while others were alert at their assigned windows. We placed hunting rifles and shotguns at each window and door along with plenty of ammo for each gun. I felt so bad that these children, as young as 10 years old, were being exposed to such fearsome circumstances, and awesome danger; but there was no alternative. Each one of them, however, seemed genuinely happy that they had their own assigned window and their own field of view to be responsible for.

Larry went to work each day at the usual time in order to maintain the appearance that all was normal at the farm. And then we waited and we waited and we waited!

His work as a law enforcement officer at the Federal Correctional Institution (FCI) in Tallahassee provided him a secure telephone with which he contacted the F.B.I.

He never told them where I was; but he told them to contact him at the FCI when they needed me and he would see to it that I was available when it was my time to testify at the trial.

Then we waited and we waited and we waited! One of us was at each window at all times, day and night. We knew that there was only one road into the farm which we could observe from the house, but we wanted an early warning signal if anyone crossed the cattle gap at the entrance to the property. Larry was skilled in the use of electronics from his Army training as a communications technician. He put this skill to good use. There was an underground telephone wire from the highway to his home which passed by a cattle gap at the entrance to his property. These lines have four wires but rarely are more than two wires used. Larry tied into the extra pair of telephone wires and connected them to the doorbell. He then rigged a tripwire across the cattle gap so that any time a vehicle crossed the cattle gap, the tripwire closed the contacts between the extra pair of wires. This then caused the doorbell to ring.

We tried it out several times and it always worked like a champ. We were happy now. We had an early warning signal when any vehicle crossed the cattle gap, entering the property. Then one night about midnight, the doorbell rang!

We all jumped up and got ready for a gunfight! We raced to our assigned windows, guns at the ready. Larry and I grabbed our weapons and slipped out the back door.

We circled around the outer edge of the farm behind the Indian Mound, and approached the cattle gap very slowly. When we got there we found the biggest raccoon you ever saw, all tangled up in the tripwire. Laughter eased the tension! We freed the raccoon and returned to the house, careful to let all the trigger happy family know we were not the bad guys.

This farm had always had a very special meaning for me. As I stared out the window toward the pasture with the cows grazing, I remembered years ago when I had been given ten days special leave from the Marine Corps before going to Vietnam War for a one year tour of Combat Duty as an A4 Fighter/Attack Jet Pilot.

What I chose to do in those ten days was to go to Larry's farm and ride his tractor. The field I was looking over from my window that day was the field I had spent those days mowing just before I left for Vietnam, and Combat.

I had grown up on a farm and loved farm life. When I was 6 years old, my Dad was a long haul truck driver. One day as he passed a group of farms near Tallahassee, he saw a sign announcing a new government project. It was 1941, and the government was trying to get people to move back to the farms and grow crops. Food was scarce and this was an effort by the Federal Government to get more farm land into production.

The government had purchased 600 acres and divided it into ten farms. On each 60 acre farm they had built a wood frame home and a barn. These farms were being offered at a very low price, if the buyer would sign a contract to actually grow crops on the land. In addition to the home and barn, the buyer received a mule with harness, and a complete set of plows, planters, and a wagon.

The purchaser had to keep records proving he was really farming the land, and selling food to wholesale buyers. If he failed to prove annually that he had produced and sold a commercial crop, the farm would be foreclosed and lost. My dad wanted one of these farms badly, but he knew that he couldn't meet all the requirements because he didn't have enough money to finance living expenses for a whole year until he could raise a crop and sell it.

Being very resourceful, Dad convinced my grandfather to agree to farm the land in a partnership while Dad continued his job, driving the long haul tractor-trailer truck. The deal was consummated and we became farmers.

All went well for two years. Then, when I was eight years old, my grandfather got the wanderlust again, and departed. That had been his pattern of life – never staying very long in one place. Dad picked up both jobs and tried to farm at night and drive his truck during the day.

One day I watched dad working on one of the plows used to cultivate the corn. The plow was very light, consisting of a main trunk with handles fastened to each side of the trunk for guiding the plow and a foot with a metal sweep attached to uproot the weeds, growing between the rows of corn.

I watched with great interest as dad removed one the two bolts holding the handles to the trunk. After he removed one bolt and loosened the other bolt, the handles could be lifted and lowered with ease. Dad then called me over and said "Son, lift and lower these handles until they feel comfortable to you." I did and when I found the spot Dad drilled a new hole through the trunk and both handles. He then replaced the second bolt. After that, he had me hitch up ole 'Mary' our mule to the plow and start plowing. Down between two rows of corn we went, cleaning out the weeds. It was one of the best feelings I ever remember as a child – total pride and joy following that mule and plowing that corn!

My older brother, Gary, and I raised and sold enough Corn to satisfy the "Feds" for the next two years. During this time, Dad was able to make enough money to pay the bills driving his long haul truck.

When WW II got really hot, Dad enlisted in the Army. After Basic Training he shipped out to the Pacific for the invasion of Japan. The war ended just before Dad's unit arrived at the Japanese Islands. Dad then went ashore with the Occupation Forces and served a year in Japan.

After the war ended Dad returned home. Because he was a War Veteran, the government waived all requirements to grow food in order to keep the property. We finally owned the farm!

We were free to stop farming if we wanted to, but I was hooked and I continued to make a crop every year until I went away to college in Columbia, SC. at age 18.

After one semester I returned to Tallahassee, enrolled at Florida State University, and continued to grow a corn crop every year until I enlisted in the U.S. Marine Corps three years later.

I had plenty of time to remember those farming years as I waited, and waited, there at Larry's farm. Waiting for the phone call from the F.B.I., I had a beautiful pasture and fond memories to enjoy while I waited.

One of those "fond memories" was the time ole Mary our mule and I were plowing the "back 40" acres. Way back in the far corner of that 40 acres were the remains of an old tobacco barn.

The previous owners had raised tobacco and used the old barn to "Flue Cure" the tobacco. The barn was two stories tall with rafters going across every 6 feet on which poles holding tobacco were placed. These poles had tobacco leaves tied to them by the stems with their leaves hanging down. Outside the barn was a fire pit with 1 foot diameter sheet metal pipes situated to carry smoke from the fire pit into the barn. This process "Flue-cured" the tobacco so it could be transported to market without spoiling.

All that was left when we acquired the property was the old shell of the barn with the old pipes lying on the dirt floor inside the barn. Around the outside of the building was the tin roof of an old porch where workers had offloaded tobacco without getting wet when it was raining.

Ole Mary and I were plowing up weeds between the rows of corn in our field near the old barn when it started raining. My dog "Pal" was with us that day, as he almost always was. Neither Mary nor I enjoyed plowing in the rain, so we took shelter in the old barn.

I got ole Mary under the tin roof and tied her to one of the support posts holding it up. Then I went inside the barn to find something fun to do while we waited for the rain to stop. Up and down the rafters I climbed pretending to be "Tarzan of the Apes".

I heard a scratching sound and looked down from a high rafter to see ole "Pal" scratching at one of the sheet metal smoke pipes, trying to get to something that was inside the pipe.

I knew ole "Pal" loved to kill snakes, and guessed that there might be a rattlesnake inside the pipe.

Hanging from the lowest rafter, I reached down and lifted one end of the pipe and "poured" the "rattlesnake" out the other end right into ole Pal's mouth. The "rattlesnake" turned out to be a huge Skunk! Pal grabbed that skunk and shook him like crazy; the way he always did when he caught a rattlesnake!

The skunk promptly sprayed me, ole Pal, and then, thru the door and all over Mary the mule!

Ole Mary took off running, taking the support pole with her. The porch roof promptly collapsed and fell over the door, trapping Pal and me, plus our skunk inside the barn.

Mom wouldn't let me in the house for weeks. I slept in the barn. I couldn't even go to school. Mom tried all the old country treatments and remedies for skunk spray; milk baths, tomato juice baths, and a few more I can't remember; but nothing worked. I just missed three weeks of school, taking several baths a day.

Yes, these were fond memories indeed, looking out that window, waiting for the Mafia to pay us a visit.

Sitting there at my assigned window, with my rifle by my side, I did a lot of soul searching and questioning my judgment for ever relating what I had seen to the FBI Agent there on River Road. Such an innocent appearing scene of two men being dropped off to go hunting, had turned out to be a complete life threatening, and life changing event for not only me, but for every member of my family.

Once I had spoken to the FBI agent, there was no way to ever return to our peaceful, normal, life.

Being in the wrong place for only 15 seconds had changed all of our worlds forever!

Chapter Five

The Trial

It was three weeks before Larry received the phone call from the F.B.I. They wanted me to go to Rome, Georgia where the trial was underway.

I was to park my car in the parking lot of the Safeway Supermarket, the only supermarket in town. Then, at a designated time, a plainclothes F.B.I. Agent would approach my car and ask if I were Rodney Letchworth. He would then show me his credentials and instruct me to get out of my car, take all my luggage and get into his car.

I had borrowed Larry's car and departed with fear and trembling on the assigned day for Rome, GA. Everything went as planned.

I ended up that night in a motel room with the best armed civilian (an F.B.I agent) I had ever encountered.

In the motel room to the right of our room, were two heavily armed F.B.I. agents, both experienced professionals. In the room to the left were two more F.B.I. agents, similarly armed.

These five agents were the most professional, best trained, group of people I have ever encountered. During the 10 days we had to wait until it was my turn to take the witness stand, we went out each day to eat using a different disguise. Some of our disguises included:

(1) We were a group of musicians returning from a concert with base horn cases, trombone cases, trumpet cases – all jam packed with pistols, rifles, and shotguns.

(2) We were a group of golfers, returning from the golf course with golf club cases all loaded with guns and ammunition.

(3) We were disguised as a group of tennis players returning from the tennis court with racket cases containing an arsenal.

No one ever suspected that these men were armed and dangerous. They were truly professionals.

Finally, it was my turn to go to the courthouse. My agents were disguised as athletes returning from the gym with large handbags, all of which were loaded with automatic pistols.

We six proceeded to the courthouse there in Rome, Ga; found the witness room and waited. Finally, the Bailiff came and escorted me to the witness stand. After being sworn in, the U.S. Attorney (The prosecutor) Craig Gillen began to question me.

This was the same Craig Gillen with whom I had spoken so many times, telling me how dangerous Michael Thevis was, and how someone in his office had "leaked" my name to one of Thevis' henchmen!

"Were you driving on River Road about 12:00 o'clock on October 25 of last year?" Mister Gillen asked. "Yes" I replied.

He then asked, "Did you see anything unusual?" I described the scene I had observed. I told the details of the Blue Mercedes Coupe with a blonde lady behind the wheel; a young man lifting a rifle out of the trunk; and a middle age man standing by the gate holding a shotgun in his left hand.

"Do you see the man in this room today whom you saw with a shotgun in his hand?" he asked. I looked at the defense table.

"That's him" I said, pointing at the defendant. At this time the idiot stood up and displayed that same open mouth grin he had displayed when I had seen him at the Gate. For some reason Thevis seemed confident that he was going to win this case.

Then Mr. Gillen said, "Let the record show that the witness has identified the defendant as the man he personally observed at the murder site only minutes before the victims were brutally murdered."

Now it was time for the cross examination! The Defense Counsel hammered me about how it could be possible for me to be so positive about my identification of the defendant when I had such a short period of time to observe the scene.

"How fast were you traveling as you passed the scene?" he asked.

I replied, "About 35 MPH".

"So", he said; "How long did you have to observe the scene traveling at that speed?"

I replied, "About 15 to 20 seconds".

He raised his voice and said, "And you want to sit there and expect us to believe that you could make a positive identification of a man you saw for less than 15 seconds. What do you do for a living?"

I answered, "Right now I am a stockbroker, but for the last 20 years I flew single seat fighter jets for the Marine Corps. At 600 MPH, 15 seconds is a lifetime.

There was quiet in the room.

I continued; "I can even tell you that he had a black curly haired wig on his head as well as that silly grin you just saw when he stood up."

The Defense Counsel sat down abruptly and there were no more questions for me. The Judge excused me from the Courtroom.

I found out later that the defense counsel was the famed Bobby Lee Cook, the Georgia Lawyer whose reputation had been the inspiration for the TV character 'Matlock'. I'm glad I didn't know about that fact on the day in question because I could not have mustered a laugh!

When I returned to the witness room looking for my five F.B.I. agents, they were nowhere to be found. The government was through with me and had discarded me like a piece of used toilet paper.

I walked all the way across town to the supermarket parking lot to retrieve Larry's car. Then I drove back across town again to the motel to retrieve my luggage. As I returned to Florida to retrieve my family, I did not have pleasant thoughts about our federal legal system.

Mob Boss Thevis had bought and owned federal employees, and could purchase any information he needed. He had purchased the information about when inmate Underhill was scheduled to show his riverfront property to innocent businessman Isaac Galanti. This info could only have been supplied by a federal employee somewhere.

Then, from someone in the office of the U.S. Attorney in Atlanta, for the Northern District of Georgia, Thevis had purchased the information that I would be a witness at his trial. Was there any hope for the legal system of our country?

The FBI Agents had disappeared after I left the Witness Room without making any arrangements for my transportation across town after giving my testimony. The Government looked to me at this time a lot like the crooks they were trying so desperately to convict!

Chapter Six

Attempted Return to Atlanta

When I arrived back at the Farm, I found two families, both ready for our family to go back to Atlanta. All the professionals we contacted believed it would be safe for us to return to Atlanta, and to our home. They believed that Thevis would not try to punish me before the trial was over because it could be used against him in the trial.

The trial was expected to last for several weeks. So we packed up and departed after thanking Larry and Rosa profusely for their hospitality and patience while they protected us from certain disaster.

On the trip back home, we speculated about what we would find when we arrived back at the house. It could have been trashed while we were gone just as a warning to me, or anything could have happened to it. Then we worried about my wife's exercise salon. Had the salon been trashed? Could she ever get her members to return? I worried about my job at Merrill Lynch. I had just disappeared without any notice. Worse yet I had not contacted my boss to inform him why I had left so suddenly and had not come back to work for more than a month.

And my investment clients! How could I ever explain why I had abandoned them with their money invested and me not there watching their investments? Worry, worry all the way home.

When we arrived home we found the house exactly as we had left it. That was a relief! The next day I found my boss very understanding. He had saved all the newspapers with stories of the trial. He had contacted all my clients with the news.

I was so relieved to find everything at work was well taken care of in my absence. I jumped right in and caught up with the market and my client's present positions. Once again I could breathe easy. My job was safe!

My wife's business was different. Many of her members were not the least bit interested in why the Salon had been closed for over a month, after they had paid their membership fees. She really had to work hard to rebuild her business.

Our children experienced some trouble returning to their schools. It seems that someone had started a rumor that I had been associated with the Mafia. Why else, the rumor went, would I have had any information about the operations which would have been of interest to a court prosecuting someone for violating the RICO (Racketeering Influenced, Corrupt Organizations) Act?

It was at this point that I learned from some friends why I had to be called to be a witness, after being told by F.B.I. agent Paul King that I did not need to worry, I would not be needed at the Trial.

According to Agent King the Feds had so many of Thevis' friends who were going to testify against him, they would not need me.

The story told me by friends working in the Fed Bureau who had knowledge of the case was this: One of the group of former associates of Thevis, who had knowledge of the crimes Thevis had committed and had agreed to tell all in exchange for The Witness Protection Program, had a strange thing happen to him shortly before the trial began.

It seems that, as he was in his second story bathroom shaving, an unusual thing happened. He was looking for a new razor blade. When he opened the door of his medicine chest on the wall above the bathroom sink, a bullet penetrated the bathroom window and shattered his reflection in the mirror.

The assassin had mistaken the reflection for the man and fired his weapon. When the news of this event spread throughout the Atlanta Mafia; all the other candidates for the Witness Protection Program developed amnesia.

The U.S. Attorney, Craig Gillen, was left with no witnesses for his trial. All he had left was the 40 hours of videotaped testimony by the murder victim, Roger Underhill telling where all the bodies were buried. Beyond that all the U.S. Attorney had was the testimony of a couple of F.B.I. agents, which wouldn't impress many jurors.

Videotape testimony in legal circles is considered "hearsay evidence" and is not admissible in a court of law.

The Constitution provides that anyone being tried in a court of law has the right to cross examine everyone who is testifying against him.

Being a very resourceful young attorney, Mr. Gillen devised a brilliant prosecution tactic. He would first try and convict Michael Thevis for the murder of Roger Underhill based on my Eyewitness Testimony alone. <u>He had no other witnesses!</u> After the murder conviction, Mr. Gillen would try and convict Thevis under the RICO statutes where he could legally take away all Thevis' ill-gotten gains (money and property).

To make this plan work, U.S. Attorney Craig Gillen got the trial judge to rule that the 40 hours of videotaped testimony by Roger Underhill was admissible hearsay evidence because the defendant Michael Thevis had been personally responsible for the witness Roger Underhill being unable to appear in court as the law required.

By this act of murdering the witness and thus preventing him from appearing in court, Michael Thevis had waived his constitutional right to cross examine Roger Underhill.

This was a new legal interpretation of existing law which was being proposed by the U.S. Attorney. Even if the Judge accepted this interpretation of the law, it would surely be appealed all the way to the Supreme Court.

Craig Gillen was successful in getting the Trial Judge to rule that Michael Thevis had waived his right to cross examine witness Roger Underhill when he murdered Underhill. Mister Gillen then presented, to the jury, 40 hours of videotaped testimony by the dead man, Roger Underhill, telling where all the bodies were buried.

As it turned out I was not the only witness who appeared in court to testify against Michael Thevis. There was a man who lived in the same neighborhood as Jeanette Evans, the blond who owned the powder blue Mercedes. He had read the Atlanta Journal the day after I testified in court. I had told about what I had witnessed at the murder scene, and had described the car and the occupants. The man recognized the car and the occupants I had described in court.

He then called the F.B.I. and told them what he had seen that same day as the murder, in his own neighborhood. One of his neighbors was a flashy young Blonde who drove a powder blue Mercedes.

On the day of the murder, he was in his yard when the young lady came home with two men in her car. One of them was a young man who was sitting in the back seat. The other man was a middle aged man of Mediterranean descent sitting in the front seat.

He went on to say that the man in front was wearing a black, curly wig. This was the exact description I had given

Paul King, F.B.I. Agent, at the scene of the crime the day of the murder, and repeated on the witness stand.

Of interest; the other witness was an Airline Pilot. The defense had a lot to say later in the appeals process about whether pilots do in fact notice small details better than average people. I don't think the matter was ever adjudicated.

We all tried our very best to return to our old lives we had enjoyed so much, but it was not to be!

We came home one day to find our furniture all shuffled with some of it in other rooms and some all busted up and scattered all over the house. I called the police and they came right over.

When I gave them my name for their report they recognized it. "Hey, aren't you the guy who testified against Thevis?" the officer asked me.

"Yes, but what does that have to do with this?" I asked.

The officer closed his book and said: "This is a Federal Case! I can't get involved. Call the F.B.I."

I called the F.B.I. When the agent answered I related to him what had happened. He said "What! Breaking and Entering! That's a matter for the local Police! Call Them!" We never got any help from any law enforcement agency! One night my wife sat up in bed and looked at the closed bedroom door. "It's all right! Come on in." She called out, thinking it was one of the children. It was an intruder! When she called out, the man ran down the stairs and out the front door. I got downstairs just in time to see him running down the street.

Then one night, I answered the phone to hear a man say, "I'm George Thevis, Michael's father. I know you must be wrong about what you said in Court about Michael. Michael could never do anything bad like that. Call the judge and tell him you made a mistake. My Michael is innocent. It's never too late to change your testimony."

I told the man that I couldn't tell a lie, and then I said "Mr. Thevis I'm very sorry but everything I said in court is the truth, the whole truth, and nothing but the truth. I'm sorry you had to hear it from me." I hung up the phone.

The harassment continued for months. Then there was the last straw! My youngest son Chuck, went into his bathroom to dress for school one morning. Our bedrooms were all on the second floor. The family room was a one story wing of the house. The peak of its roof was level with the upstairs bath which Chuck was using.

When Chuck looked out his bathroom window he saw a man with a shotgun sitting on the roof of the family room, only 10 feet from the bathroom window. Chuck came screaming into my bedroom! I ran to see what was happening. I got to the bathroom just in time to see the man jump off the roof and run away across the yard.

I called the police who told me to call the F.B.I. So I called the F.B.I. who told me to call the Police. We could not get help from any Law Enforcement Agency. This was the last straw for me.

I put the house on the market and told my boss I would be leaving as soon as the house sold. He was very understanding and asked me where I was planning to move.

I said, "Tallahassee, that's where most of my relatives live." He said "I'll call the Merrill Lynch Manager there. You'll have a job waiting when you arrive." I thanked him and started planning the move.

My oldest daughter Terrie, had met a fine young man and they were talking about marriage. She wanted to get married in the front yard of our beautiful home before we sold it. She and her mother planned the wedding and the ceremony was conducted right there in the front yard. The home sold shortly thereafter and we packed up and left for Florida.

Chapter Seven

Second Flight to Florida

All the trauma of the Trial and the aftermath of the threats had left me emotionally drained. I had always enjoyed working with my hands. Activities such as woodworking, masonry, electrical installation, plumbing etc. had been the skills I had acquired while I worked my way through college.

I decided I would buy a 100 year old home in downtown Monticello, Florida. The house needed lots of love and care. It also needed lots of paint and repair. I figured this repair project would help restore my sanity and be a fun project to keep me busy so I could forget Michael Thevis and the Mob. The house had been built in 1905 on the site of a previous home which had burned down the year before. In those days all cooking was done on wood burning stoves. Frequently, sparks from the wood burning stoves would escape and ignite the wood building. The popular home design of those days placed the kitchen in a separate building from the main house. The two structures were connected by a covered wooden walkway. When the kitchen caught fire and burned, the main house was spared.

In the case of my old house, the previous house had caught fire and burned to the ground, leaving the kitchen standing. So, when the new house was built in 1905, they left the old kitchen, built a new home and attached the two with a covered wooden walkway.

When we bought the property, we purchase a 100 year old mansion with a 150 year old attached kitchen. I spent many happy hours restoring the old home to its previous grandeur.

I even took a Stained Glass course so I could repair the damage in the stained glass around the front door. I really enjoyed that part of my project!

My son, Chuck became an avid duck hunter. I had some oak flooring boards left over from replacing the floor in the living room, so I made Chuck a gun cabinet with them. For the gun cabinet doors I used some of my stained glass to create a scene with ducks flying in formation. Then I framed the glass with oak flooring lumber. Chuck still has this cabinet in his family room today.

The 25 mile commute to and from Tallahassee each day provided lots of time to plan my strategy for finding new clients and building my business as a Merrill Lynch Broker. Things went well at work and my client base grew exponentially.

Once again, life was great! During this time my younger daughter, Patti had maintained a correspondence with a young man she had met in Atlanta. She and Larry decided to get married.

The ceremony was conducted in our beautiful front yard with a beautifully restored 100 year old mansion for a background. After the wedding, she and Larry moved to Houston, TX where his family lived and where he had a job waiting. Life was great again. But that was about to change!

One day I received a phone call at my office from Craig Gillen, the U.S. Attorney who had prosecuted Michael Thevis at the trial in Rome, Georgia.

After the pleasantries he asked "Mr. Letchworth, do you have a daughter?" I replied "Yes, I have two daughters; one lives in Houston, and the other lives there in Atlanta."

He then asked "The one who lives in Atlanta: Where is she right now?" I replied, "Well, she works at Jilly's Restaurant so I suppose that's where she would be right now." There was a pause and then he almost shouted "My God! Thevis owns that place! We have information from a source that Thevis is planning to kidnap her, and hold her for ransom until you agree to change your testimony." His appeals are not going well for him right now, and he wants to do something drastic."

I replied, "Mr. Gillen, I'm leaving for Atlanta right now and <u>I will take care of this</u>. Thank you for giving me the information! I'll take care of it!"

I hung up the phone, told my boss I had to leave and I didn't know when I would be back.

Then I raced home, loaded all the guns and ammo I had into the car, went by the bank and withdrew all the cash I had in my account and left town headed for Atlanta.

When I arrived at Jilly's I went inside and found Terrie. We went out to the car and I told her the news.

Then I said to her: "You are not going back into that building!"

"We are going to Terry's workplace right now. (Daughter Terrie had married a man name Terry. Their friends called them "Y" and "IE").

We found Terry at work. I told him the news. Then I gave him my 45 caliber pistol, all my ammo, all the money I had. I told them to get out of town quickly and go to

Houston, TX, and stay with Pattie and Larry until it was safe to come back to Atlanta.

WOW! Would this nightmare ever end? Shortly after this episode Shearson Leamon/American Express opened a Brokerage office in Tallahassee. They were looking for local stockbrokers to grow their business.

One day I received a call from their branch manager asking me to join him for lunch. The routine was the same as last time, except that this time the offer was off the page!

I was offered a Salary of $10,000.00 a month for ONE YEAR. This was 1984. Such money was unbelievable! Needless to say I accepted the offer and moved to my new office.

Sometimes money can go to your head. This was one time when it did. I bought a 7 acre lot on a lake in the best part of town. Then I built a 5200 sq. ft., two story home with columns across the front. We moved from

Monticello to our new home on the lake in Tallahassee. Life was great. But only for a while.

<u>All this was about to change!</u>

Chapter Eight

Mafia Hit Contract

The Witness Protection Program

Late one evening as I was engrossed in an exciting program on TV, the phone rang. When I answered, there was a voice on the line that said, "Mister Letchworth this is the F.B.I. We have just recorded a phone conversation between Michael Thevis in the Federal Prison in Marion, IL; and one of his associates.

Thevis issued a contract with this man to have you killed! We believe that you should start carrying a gun at all times, and exercise extreme caution. This is a very serious matter. Please do not take it lightly. If you see or hear anything unusual, please contact your local law enforcement officials."

"What are <u>you</u> going to do?" I asked in a desperate voice.

"There is nothing we <u>can</u> do" he replied, "We are only funded to investigate crimes and prosecute criminals; we are not funded to prevent crimes. Contact your local law enforcement officials". The line went dead as he hung up.

The next morning I called the U.S. Attorney, Craig Gillen, in Atlanta. When he came on the line I repeated my conversation of the previous evening with the F.B.I. agent.

There was a long silence on the line. Then he said, "Mr. Letchworth, Mike Thevis has waited for more than 4 years for his conviction to be appealed all the way to the Supreme Court.

During this time he has done nothing to harm you for fear it would endanger his chances of winning an appeal. This was a new law which we created and the Supreme Court has just affirmed it. Never before has "Hearsay Evidence" been admissible in court.

Last week the Supreme Court affirmed his conviction and his sentence. Now he must spend the rest of his life in prison without any possibility of parole. You must take this threat seriously. He has nothing to lose. Be careful!"

I asked, "What are you going to do?"

He replied, "Nothing, we are not funded to prevent crimes, we are only funded to prosecute crimes. Contact your local law enforcement agents. I'm very sorry!"

"Well", I said, "when we first talked, back before the trial, you promised me that if things got really bad, you would get me into the Witness Protection Program. I'm ready to take you up on that offer now."

There was a long pause before he spoke. Then he said, "Mr. Letchworth, I am so sorry to tell you this, but when I made that promise, I thought I had the authority to make it. Now I find that I do not have that authority. I cannot help you!"

It seemed unbelievable to me that a criminal could get protection from the Mob through The Witness Protection Program, and an honest citizen was not eligible for help.

This had to be a mistake! I decided I would talk to our local Congressman, Don Fuqua for assistance in getting into the Federal Witness Protection Program.

The next morning I went to the Congressman's office in Tallahassee and told him the whole sordid story. He asked me to give him time and he would find out what was going on at the Justice Department. This was on a Thursday.

Two days later, on a Saturday afternoon, two men appeared at my front door and knocked. I invited the men in after they showed me their credentials. They were Federal Marshals.

They informed me that they were there to take me into the Witness Protection Program! These men were surly, impolite, and demanding.

When I told them I only had twenty dollars in my pocket, they told me I wouldn't need any money; they were going to provide everything I needed.

At the airport I was handed a ticket from Tallahassee to Atlanta, and instructed to be the last passenger to get off the plane in Atlanta. My plane reservation had been made using a fake identity.

In Atlanta I was the last passenger to get off the plane. A man approached me and asked if I was Rodney Letchworth. I said yes. He showed me his credentials which identified him as a U.S. Marshall, and then said "Follow me". I followed him to another terminal where he handed me a ticket and told me to be the last passenger to get off the plane after it landed in Washington, D.C.

When I arrived in Washington, I was the last one to get off the plane and the procedure was the same as in Atlanta. The Marshall said, "Follow me". I followed him to a car outside where another surly agent was waiting.

I found out later why all six of the U.S. Marshall's were unhappy. Their weekend activities had been disrupted and they resented me for causing their holiday fun to be disturbed. Congressman Fuqua must have raised Hell with someone in The Justice Department.

The Marshals drove all over Washington, going from the airport to the far northeast part of town. Then they drove south into Virginia. Then we went northwest into Maryland. They were constantly looking over their shoulder. Finally they stopped in front of a ragged, rundown hotel in northwestern Bethesda, Maryland.

I was seated in the back seat, and the two Marshalls were in the front seat. The passenger side agent turned in his seat and handed me a key. "You are registered here as Raymond Franklin. We've already checked you in, and the room is paid for. Stay here until we come back. Until then, don't speak to anyone. NOT ANYONE!! Michael Thevis has an army looking for you, and he's mad as hell! Don't use any phone to call anyone you know. He has all their phones tapped. Don't use any of your credit cards.

He can track you from that. Don't cash a check. If you do, he'll find you. Just be quiet and wait for us to come back."

"But," I cried out: "I have no money. Your agents in Tallahassee would not let me go to the bank before we left Tallahassee! I only have $20 in my pocket!"

"Don't worry," he said. "We'll be back before you run out of money, just stay quiet and don't attract any attention."

I got out of the car and carried my one small bag into the hotel and straight up to my room. I had no idea how long I would have to wait so I decided to eat light. I limited my food to one hamburger a day from the McDonald's down the street.

With so much time to think, I began to reminisce about the three years I had lived in Potomac, Maryland, not more than ten miles from this "flea bag" hotel where I was now staying. I had served 21 years in the Marine

Corps, and three of those years had been right here in Washington D.C. at Marine Corps Headquarters.

My office was located only a few blocks from The Pentagon. My assignment at Marine Headquarters was, "Head of Marine Aviation Studies and Analysis". This was a "payback assignment" for having had the privilege of attending the Naval Postgraduate School at Monterey, California for two years and acquiring a Graduate Degree In "Operations Research and Systems Analysis".

I had always enjoyed mathematics and science courses in high school and the three years I attended Florida State University before enlisting in the Marine Corps. In boot camp at Parris Island, SC, I applied for Flight School and was accepted. In Flight School at Pensacola, Florida I excelled!

I finished Preflight School with the highest grade point average ever recorded for a Naval Aviation Cadet. (My record stood for 10 years.) I had my choice of aircraft schools and selected Jet Fighters. I graduated from Flight School and received my Wings and Commission as a

Second Lieutenant in the U.S. Marine Corps on September 9th 1959.

My first squadron assignment was with the "Blacksheep" Squadron, VMA 214, located at Marine Corps Airbase, Kaneohe Bay, Hawaii.

Life in Hawaii was grand! The weather, the beaches, the mountains, the flying were all fabulous.

Our squadron mission was "Nuclear Weapons Delivery". It was 1959 and the United States was in a "nuclear standoff" with Russia and China. All our Long Range Nuclear Missiles on the East Coast of the US were aimed at Russia. In the Pacific our nuclear assets were not missiles – they were Nuclear Bombs which could only be delivered by aircraft. Our Nuclear Weapons Delivery Aircraft was the FJ4B (Fury Jet).

Our weapon was a 2.5 megaton thermonuclear bomb. It was equivalent in explosive power to 150 bombs the size of one of the two dropped on Japan during WWII.

With such powerful explosives, normal conventional weapons delivery techniques were not appropriate. There would not have been enough separation between the aircraft and the bomb at detonation to assure survival of the aircraft and crew.

To solve this dilemma new delivery techniques had been developed. These techniques involved "throwing the bomb" and using the time the bomb was in "free flight" to maneuver the aircraft in such a manner as to get the maximum distance between the bomb and the aircraft at the time of detonation. The maneuver used by the "Blacksheep" squadron was named "Over the Shoulder" maneuver.

In this maneuver the aircraft performs a normal "loop", starting at 50 feet above the ground traveling at 500 knots (app 650 mph). The loop is started directly over the target using a four 'g' pull up.

At 90 degrees (vertical) the aircraft has gone approximately five miles beyond the target. At 130 degrees the weapon is released, and the pilot continues in the four "G" loop. The weapon goes up to 18,000 feet and then arcs back the five miles to the target.

The aircraft continues its four "G" maneuver until it is pointed down at 45 degrees below the horizon, headed away from the target. At this point the pilot rolls the Aircraft 180 degrees and continues down and directly away from the target.

The aircraft continues down to 50 feet above the terrain, full throttle, and headed directly away from the target.

This delivery maneuver results in the aircraft achieving 15 to 20 nautical miles separation from the target when the bomb detonates.

We nicknamed this maneuver the "Idiot Loop". (You have to inject some levity into the conversation when talking about stressful and dangerous activity.)

While I sat in my room at the "fleabag hotel" there in Bethesda, Maryland, I reminisced about those good ole days. Flying "Idiot Loops" every day and competing with my squadron mates on our bombing scores.

We used inert, practice bombs on a target island off the northeast end of Hawaii's Oahu Island, the main Island in the Hawaiian chain of Islands.

We had a spotter plane circling the target to call our hits. I got the nickname "Kentucky Windage" in the Blacksheep Squadron. This was because I had been a rifle instructor for a year at Parris Island while waiting to go to Flight School. Ordinarily, wind is compensated for by moving the rifle's rear sight left or right as many 'clicks' as needed to compensate for the estimated wind speed.

Flags on each side of the target range assist the shooter in guessing the wind speed. If you don't have movable sights, you correct for wind by just aiming to the left or right of the target. This practice is nicknamed "Kentucky Windage". The name is really a derogatory phrase, implying that there are no rifles with moveable sights in Kentucky.

We were discussing how to correct for wind in our "Idiot Loop" bombing. I had the best CEP (Circular Error Probability) score in our squadron. When the guys asked me how I did it, I told them, "I use "Kentucky Windage". I was compensating for wind by adjusting my pull up point into the wind, not starting directly over the target and compensating for wind by dropping a wing into the wind as we had been trained to do. So I got the nickname "Kentucky Windage". The other guys were passing directly over the target and then dropping a wing into the wind after starting their pull up; a much less accurate technique.

I passed the time in the "flea bag hotel", reliving many of my childhood and early adult years. I was very awkward and uncoordinated as a teenager. I shot up to six feet tall before I was 14 years old.

It wasn't until I reached 21 that my coordination caught up with my height which had increased to 6'4". In addition to being awkward, I was also very shy, especially around girls. This probably contributed to my love of farming. Plowing that old mule and later on plowing with our tractor probably were activities I used to give me excuses for missing most of the social activities in our neighborhood and at school.

I did love plowing with that ole mule, and driving the small tractor Daddy bought after he returned from the war. When I was a senior in high school my grandfather had returned from his wandering and had bought a country store and gas station a couple of miles from the Indian Mound.

He had five acres behind the store and wanted me to plant it in corn for him. I loaded the tractor on our trailer, and drove the ten miles from our home to his store. It took me two weeks to plow the ground and plant the corn.

I stayed with him and rode the school bus to and from school until I finished the job. It was on a Saturday, April 1st, 1953 that I finished planting, loading the tractor on the trailer, and driving back to our farm.

That night shortly after I left, Grandfather was closing up for the night when an escaped convict sneaked up behind him and shot him in the head with a shotgun. Then the convict and another convict, who had escaped with him, stole everything they could get into their stolen car and left.

One of the items they took was my grandfather's shotgun. Two weeks later when the convicts were captured, they still had my grandfather's shotgun.

Before the trial of these convicts I was asked to come to the courthouse to speak to the Prosecuting Attorney. He was having trouble finding evidence to prove that these were in fact the men who had killed my grandfather.

He asked me if I could positively identify the shotgun that was found with the suspects when they were captured. He wanted to know why I was so sure that this was Granddaddy's shotgun. That was easy for me because this shotgun had a peculiar feature not found on many shotguns.

When the gun was broken down to reload, it would forcefully 'eject' the spent shell casing. I had found out the hard way that it was necessary to hold the gun pointed to the left or the empty shell would hit me in the face. I demonstrated it to the Prosecuting Attorney, using an empty shell. The shell was ejected about six feet to my right. The prosecutor was delighted.

He then had me appear on the witness stand at the trial and demonstrate it for the Jury. The demonstration convinced the Jury that the shotgun found with these men was the one which had been stolen from my grandfather the night they killed him.

The sentence for both men was death in the electric chair.

This had been a most traumatic experience for me, and I had somehow managed to keep it out of my conscious mind for those many years until I found myself once again being the key witness at another murder trial.

There were also <u>pleasant</u> memories during this time from my youth. One summer, my friend Nakomas and I were earning money harvesting Bahia grass seeds on the largest plantation in the county. Konie was driving the tractor and I was bagging seeds on the combine.

Suddenly a baby deer jumped up from the grass directly in front of me and took off running. I yelled at Konie to stop! Then we both took off running and finally caught the young fellow.

We put him in one of the seed bags, with only his head sticking out. We then tied him in securely.

With him thus bound up, we deposited him under a tree beside the paved road we used to go home after work.

I lived closer to town than Konie did so we thought it would be safer for "Buck" to live with Konie.

Buck became a family pet. He grazed in the pasture with the cows during the day, and came back to the barn at night. He recognized me when I came to visit and would come running to get his head petted.

After several years Buck had grown quite a large rack of antlers. We began to worry that a hunter might come by the farm, see Buck in the pasture with the cows, and think he was a wild deer.

It would have been a tempting target for any avid hunter. So we decided that for Buck's sake we should get him to some safer place.

When we had been working down in South Florida during the previous summer, we had passed a Park between Tallahassee and Tampa which had a natural spring (Homosassa Springs) and a "Petting Zoo" with wild animals.

We decided that this would be a good, safe home for Buck. So I hitched up the old trailer, which I had hauled the tractor around on, and went to Konie's.

We loaded Buck into the trailer securely, and took him to his new home down the state. He became the major attraction at the zoo. We stopped to visit him on every trip for many years. He recognized us and eagerly came running when he saw us coming.

Then I remembered some of the exciting times I had experienced while flying those single seat fighter jets. One summer our FJ4B Nuclear Weapons Delivery fighter Jet squadron based in Hawaii was deployed to Yuma, Arizona for Low Level Navigation Training.

Prior to this deployment we had not received any navigation training of any kind while stationed at Kaneohe Bay, Hawaii. All our training had been in nuclear weapons delivery techniques.

Our mission called for us to be prepared at all times to deploy on an aircraft carrier from somewhere near Hawaii; ride west on the carrier to a pre-assigned location in the Pacific Ocean. After arriving at the assigned location, we would be launched with a nuclear weapon aboard our little bird and be expected to deliver it to an assigned target somewhere in Asia, never getting above 50 feet from the earth's surface.

Low level navigation over long distances is very difficult due to the short line-of-sight distance available. Over water we just flew a predetermined heading, but over land there are opportunities for course corrections computed from landmarks identified.

We needed to get some practice flying over land at 50' altitude constantly making course corrections from information obtained by identifying the terrain features we were passing, and finding these features on our map.

We were scheduled and deployed as a squadron from Hawaii to MCAS Yuma, Arizona for three months assigned training. The training routes required special approval from the Federal Aviation Administration.

There were also requirements to have a 'chase pilot' at 200' altitude, following the low level pilot who would be flying at 50'.

The 'chase pilot' was responsible for keeping the 50' pilot from getting 'lost', or straying too far off course. He was also responsible for spotting 'high voltage electric power lines', and warning the low level pilot when he was approaching one.

The assigned, approved route went from Yuma, Arizona east and then northeast several hundred miles; then north several hundred miles; then southwest several hundred miles; then west several hundred miles out over the Pacific Ocean; then south a relatively short distance before reversing back east to Yuma. Flying at 50 and without any electronic navigation aids was a terribly difficult assignment.

Several memorable events happened while I was on this deployment. The first occurred the first week we were in the air. There were numerous large farms in the valleys around Yuma. That first week we were in the air, the Air Station Commander got a phone call from a very irate local farmer. It seems that one of our planes had flown under one of his 'crop duster' planes while the 'crop duster' was dusting crops. The culprit was identified as a Marine fighter jet! We got a very stern warning from our Squadron Commander. It went something like this: "OK men, ten feet over water around Hawaii is one thing, but here over land, the minimum is 50 feet. Does everyone understand me?"

In Hawaii we had practiced our low level delivery maneuvers over the water and had become comfortable flying very low. Before this incident we hadn't realized that our 50 feet had become closer to 10 feet.

The next event occurred when I was 'chasing' my friend Dondy. After Dondy topped a mountain ridge in Northern Arizona at 50 feet, he called, "Rod, do you know where we are?" "Sure Dondy, why do you ask?" "Well", he said; "Mark it on your map. I might need to know later".

We proceeded with our assignment and returned home after completing the mission. Dondy was slow getting out of his bird after his flight, so I walked over to the plane to wait for him.

Then I saw it. The entire front half of his "Shape" (his practice nuclear bomb which was the exact shape, size and weight of the real nuclear weapon which we were practicing to deliver) was missing!

He had hit a tall Pine tree as he topped the ridge and had lost the entire front of his 'Shape'. There were green pine needle markings all over both the top and bottom of his wing. I shuddered as I slowly realized how very close I had come to losing my wingman.

All I would have had to remember him by would have been my map where I had marked the spot.

There were no eventful episodes when I flew my 'Low Level Navigation Training Flight'. However, the next low level training flight which I chased at 200 feet, came close to being my last flight as a 'Marine Aviator'!

I was chasing my friend "Sal" (short for Salvatore). Sal did very well until we were flying west, approaching a 15 degree turn to the south. We were about 50 miles east of the California coast. Sal had his map folded accordion style, as we all did, however his fold was right at the 15 degree turn. When he turned his map over, he missed the turn. Well I caught it but I waited some minutes to see if he would catch the error himself. BIG MISTAKE!

I finally called it to his attention, but too late to keep us from flying directly over the Marine Corps Air Station at El Toro, California.

Sal was at 50 feet, and I was at 200 feet as we crossed the field. There were aircraft at the 'Break' at 1000 feet overhead, but they were of no concern to us.

What had our attention was a small, two engine Beechcraft which was making an approach on the crosswind runway from our left at 200 feet.

Sal dropped to treetop height to avoid hitting the Beechcraft. I was at 200 feet, level with the Beechcraft. With traffic above at 1000 feet, I decided to follow Sal down and go under the Beechcraft.

We both crossed the golf course at treetop height, right over the 8th tee of the base golf course. It was our luck that the Commanding General of the Air Wing was just teeing off, and man did he get TEED OFF!

The General preferred charges against us under the Uniform Code of Military Justice, and scheduled a General Court-martial. The NCIS was called in to investigate the incident. Sal and I were arrested by the Military Police when we got out of our aircraft at Yuma. We were then transported to MCAS El Toro to await trial.

We were confined to the BOQ (Bachelor Officer Quarters) at El Toro during the two weeks of the investigation. When the investigation was complete, we were called in to the General Court-martial office to hear the results of the NCIS investigation.

The NCIS Officer in charge of the investigation reported that he had concluded that we were not at fault in being over the airport when the incident occurred. He accepted our explanation about the fold in the map resulting in a navigation error.

However, he could find no reason for us to be at treetop heights. There were no records of a Beechcraft landing at the airbase on that day, so we should have been at our assigned altitudes of 50 feet for Sal, and 200 feet for me.

His recommendation was that we have our designations as Naval Aviators revoked. (Take our wings away and ground us forever)!

The Officer in Charge of the Court-martial asked if we had any comments.

I got up and protested that there had in fact been a Beechcraft in an approach to land, and that if we hadn't taken evasive action, there would have been a collision. I further stated that it appeared to me that the Beechcraft had been making a Ground Controlled Approach (GCA) to the off duty runway, because the other traffic had been landing on a different runway.

I asked the investigating officer if he had checked the records of the Ground Controlled Approach department. He replied that he had not.

The Officer in Charge of the court-martial then ordered the NCIS Officer to check the GCA records and report back the results.

When the court-martial was reconvened, the NCIS Officer reported that the records had shown that there had indeed been a Beechcraft from Miramar Naval Air Station practicing GCA approaches that day.

He further stated that he had interviewed the pilots of the Beechcraft and they had praised our actions as having been necessary to prevent a midair Collison.

We were exonerated of the charges, and ordered to report back to our squadron for full duty.

WOW! Was that a close call? Now back to Hawaii and flying those 'Idiot Loops'.

What pleasant memories I enjoyed as I waited for the U. S. Marshalls to come and put me into the Witness Protection Program there in Washington, D.C. When I enlisted in the U.S. Marine Corps in 1956, I had outgrown my awkwardness but was still very shy and unsure of myself. I will never forget my Drill Instructor, Gunnery Sergeant Herbert Bratcher. He changed my life forever! '

'Gunny' Bratcher was demanding, never accepting anything but perfection. His motto was: "In the Marine Corps, we do difficult things immediately! Impossible things take a little longer, 'but By Damn' we get them done too". By this time my coordination had caught up with my height, and my work on the farm all those years had left me very strong.

All of us recruits were pushed to perform beyond our capacity. Most of us began to realize that our capacity to perform was well beyond what we ever thought it was.

The more Gunny Bratcher pushed me, the more I began to realize that I could do anything I set my mind to. This realization had changed my life into something I never thought could happen to me. I credit this man for most of the accomplishments I have achieved in my life.

Trying to become a "Marine" was a test of every talent and strength I had in my body. Upon graduation, I was named 'Recruit of The Year' and awarded a brand new Marine Corps Dress Blue Uniform.

Finding that I had excelled in earning that title of "Marine" had given me the confidence to try and achieve everything else that I have found to be a desirable pursuit. And then t Gunny told us that we should never use the term "Ex-Marine"! There may come a day when you are not on active duty but once you become a Marine, you are "Always a Marine!" That's how I have survived this "Witness" episode in my life. I give Gunnery Sergeant Bratcher credit for preparing me for all the trials I have survived.

Here I was in a "flea bag hotel" waiting for two U.S. Marshals to return and finish putting me into the Witness Protection Program!

I had only eaten one hamburger at McDonald's each day. I began to hope for the day when I could a buy a coke and French Fries also. Only one hamburger a day was all I allowed myself to eat. It was a good thing I had because I ran out of money after eight days.

I waited two more days without anything to eat. At that point I got Mad. And then I got really mad! Finally, after 12 days of waiting I decided to do something about it.

I packed my suitcase and left that rundown, rat infested hotel and walked to the nearest bank. There I cashed a check. I was elated to have money in my pocket again. I then stopped at McDonald's, and celebrated with a real meal, complete with french-fries and a coke.

Thus fortified with some food, I caught the Metro to Downtown D.C.

There I found directions to the Justice Department building. I told the security guard at the entrance that I had been a witness in a high profile case in Atlanta and I needed to speak to the official here in Washington who was the supervisor of Craig Gillen, the U.S. Attorney in Atlanta. I wanted to lodge a complaint against Mr. Gillen.

The security guard took my name and went over to a small room and spoke to his supervisor. The supervisor made a few phone calls, and then he came over and gave me directions to a Deputy Attorney General's office on the 2th floor. After a 20 minute wait in the hallway I was escorted into a massive conference room. There I found a conference table about 15 feet long with 7 chairs centered on one side of the table and one chair centered on the other side. I was directed to sit in the single seat, facing the seven people on the other side of the table. All of the people across from me had worried looks on their faces.

Finally the lady in the middle spoke. She introduced herself and then said "I'm the Deputy Attorney General of the United States. First I want to thank you Mr. Letchworth for your help in convicting a very dangerous and vicious criminal.

Your testimony at his trial was the key evidence that led to his conviction for murder and violations of the RICO Act (Racketeering Influenced Corrupt Organization). He was given a life sentence without parole. All of his assets were confiscated by the government. We thought we had put him out of business for good.

But, I have bad news for you Mr. Letchworth. Three months ago an Appellate Judge ruled that we could only legally confiscate the assets which he had accumulated while committing the crimes for which we convicted him. All the other assets which he had accumulated in the acts for which we did not have enough evidence to charge him, we were forced to return to him.

He now has $100 Million in assets and a bank account with $50 Million in it. As we speak, he has an army of lawyers, flying coast to coast every day, trying to find any way to get him out of prison.

You must know, Mr. Letchworth that he is a very dangerous man, and you are in grave danger wherever you go. We suggest you get a permit and carry a weapon with you at all times."

After a few minutes of stunned silence I asked "What are _you_ going to do? The U.S. Attorney in Atlanta, Craig

Gillen, promised before the trial that if I ever needed it, he would get me into the Witness Protection Program. I'm ready to get in right now."

The Deputy Attorney General of the United States said: "Mr. Letchworth, I'm so very sorry to have to tell you, but we cannot get you into the Witness Protection Program. Mr. Gillen is a young Attorney General and he thought he had the authority to make that promise, but he didn't.

The Witness Protection Program is only funded to protect 'indicted' criminals who agree to provide testimony needed to convict their mob bosses.

You are an unindicted, innocent witness. We have no funds to provide security for you."

The room was as silent as a tomb. Not a word was spoken for several minutes. Then they all got up and walked slowly and quietly out of the room.

I was stunned! For a long time, I just sat there alone, in that huge, quiet, room. It was disgraceful for our government to provide hundreds of millions of dollars a year to protect an indicted criminal; and not have even one penny to protect an honest innocent citizen who had risked his life to put a Mafia boss behind bars for life. It was more than I could accept.

I left the Department of Justice building and went over to the Senate Office Building. There I asked to see Senator Sam Nunn. This crime had occurred in Georgia which was his state. Sen. Nunn received me graciously. After a short friendly chat, I explained my dilemma.

Sen. Nunn told me about the investigation of the Witness Protection Program he had just completed. His investigation had uncovered an incredible list of incidents where the Marshals Service agents had sold information to the Mob, resulting in the death of witnesses and their families.

Since no one knew the real names of these dead witnesses there were no repercussions against the U.S. Marshals who were supposed to have been protecting the witnesses. Sen. Nunn gave me a copy of his investigation and congratulated me on NOT BEING ABLE TO GET INTO the Witness Protection Program!

I left his office stunned, unable to believe what I had heard. Here in the United States of America, why would our government treat a Combat Veteran in such a shameful fashion?

I went to the airport and used my credit card to buy a ticket home. I was glad to be out of that pit of vipers who were running our country. The next day I visited Congressman Don Fuqua in Tallahassee to thank him for his help and give him the copy of Sen. Nunn's investigation into the Witness Protection Program. I was ready to forget about any government help and find my own way to survive.

Chapter Nine

Flight to Coral Gables

I could not stay in Tallahassee and just wait for the Mafia hit man to earn his money. I would be endangering anyone else near me at the time of the hit. Besides, I wouldn't have been able to concentrate on any work.

I knew that I couldn't be effective as a stockbroker, so I notified my boss at Shearson/Lehman that I would not be returning to the office. I thanked him profusely for his generosity, and wished him well.

I knew that I could not pay mortgage payments on two homes from just my military pension alone.

I moved my family back to Monticello and into the restored, 100 year old Mansion, which had the smaller mortgage.

Then I said goodbye to my wife and children; got in my car and left town, not knowing where in the world I would end up.

I ended up in Coral Gables, about 400 miles from home! There I found a job working in a securities firm whose only product was selling option contracts on gold futures.

These investments were highly speculative and produced either a fabulous return, or a devastating loss. My job consisted of writing and entering the clients buy and sell orders.

It was a low paying job, but I was able to keep up the payments on both homes and send some money home to supplement the monthly military pension payments which were being automatically deposited into my bank account in Monticello for my family there.

I could never relax though. I remained in my apartment at all times when I was not working. I never used the phones, either in the apartment or at work, to call home. The stress of this isolation began to cause psychological problems.

I started having flashbacks to Vietnam!

My job in the war was flying the A4 Skyhawk Aircraft, providing close air support to Marine and Army ground forces. Although the A4 was initially designed to deliver nuclear weapons, we found that it was superbly suited for this mission of close air support! The bird was small and nimble (maneuverable).

As a standard load, the A4 carried six 500 pound bombs, ten 250 pound bombs, two 44 gallon napalm canisters, and two 20m millimeter canons with 100 rounds of ammunition each.

Close air support is usually performed when the ground forces get into a situation where they are outnumbered and need help. This was the case for almost every engagement in Vietnam. The NVA (North Vietnamese Army) never initiated an engagement unless they had the high ground and a superior force of troops.

By the time we arrived on the scene, the space between our forces and the NVA was frequently less than 50 meters (150 feet). Our weapons delivery had to be extremely accurate or our own troops could be injured.

We had special fins on our bombs which deployed when the bomb was released. Their fins acted as 'speed brakes' to slow the bomb's forward motion.

These bombs we nicknamed "Snakeye Bombs". They allowed us to release very low above the target. Our standard release point was 50 feet above the terrain, 350 knots (400 mph), in a 15 degree dive and on a heading which kept us from flying over our troops.

During my 11 months in country, I flew 289 combat missions. I was very fortunate to return home <u>without</u> a Purple Heart medal! Many of my friends were not so lucky. My Skyhawk, however, qualified for a Purple Heart on almost every mission.

Our "metal benders" (airframe repair mechanics) had plenty of work digging bullets out of our birds after almost every flight. They were great men to have on our team. Every morning they would present us with our souvenirs (mangled bullets which they had dug out of our bird). When I came home I brought a box full of them with me.

We seldom knew when we left our base exactly where we would be working. This information was passed to us by Forward Air Controllers (FAC's). Usually these FAC's were airborne in small, light observation aircraft, but occasionally the FAC's were on the ground accompanying the troops we were assigned to support, or separate "Sniper Units" who were primarily "Intelligence Gatherers" When they discovered a significantly important target, they had proper radio equipment to call in an airstrike. We loved working with these guys because they were truly professionals, and were always able to guide us to significant targets.

After we arrived in the area of operations, we would establish communications with our FAC or Sniper contact by checking in with him on an assigned radio frequency. He would then brief us on the ground situation and describe the target he wanted us to destroy. If the FAC was airborne and the target was very close to our ground forces, the FAC would "mark" the target by firing a smoke rocket. Then he would identify the target's exact location by how far and in which direction the target was located from his "smoke".

Our mission was "close air support". There were occasions when it was necessary for me to drop bombs on targets as close as 50 meters (half the length of a football field) from our troops. I always worried about our young men being tempted to lift their heads and watch the "air show". This could have been fatal because an exploding 500 lb. bomb sends shrapnel flying in all directions, and it was crucial that our guys keep their heads down!

As one can imagine our "targets" were firing at us fast and furiously as we passed their position at 400 MPH. Frequently they were lucky, and our "metal benders" had some business when we got back home.

After we ran out of bombs, napalm, and ammo we would ask our FAC if he had another flight inbound. If he didn't, we asked if he had the situation under control or if we could help by making dummy runs. Some battles were so fierce that we would make a dummy run every 2nd or 3rd pass just to keep the enemy guessing whether we had any ammo left or not. We did this to protect the troops until help arrived. It was always dangerous making dummy runs, especially dangerous if you really didn't have any ammo left.

I was there during the 'TET OFFENSIVE'; the 'BATTLE of HUE'; the 'BATTLE of KHE SANH'; and the 'BATTLE OF A SHAU VALLEY'! (1967-1968)!

Chapter Ten

Flashbacks to Combat
PTSD Rears its Ugly Head
Five Months in a Psychiatric Ward

So here I am in Coral Gables; afraid to leave my room; constantly watching over my shoulder for the Mafia hit man; mad as hell at the U. S. Government for their refusal to help me in any way.

Every day, I was experiencing flashbacks to combat! I began to feel guilt about killing all those people. I thought about the first mission I flew when I knew that I would probably kill some innocent peasants.

I was tasked to bomb a village where intelligence had reported a very large force of NVA. There was a report that leaflets had been dropped over the village advising the residents to evacuate because the village was going to be destroyed.

As I orbited the village, I thought about the small villages around where I had grown up. People there included many of my relatives. Some of them would have been too stubborn to evacuate. There probably are people just like that living it this village, I thought.

I asked myself, "Do you really want to kill all these people?" I am a Christian. I try to follow the Commandments. The Good Book says, "Thou shall not kill". I was about to kill a lot of people!

So I faced that moment of truth in the cockpit. I knew that I could just jettison my bombs out over the water, go back to the base and turn in my wings. Sure, I could just be a trash collector for the rest of my tour. A Lieutenant Colonel had done just that a month before. He now walks around the base in total disgrace. It was a moment of truth for me.

Then it was my turn to roll in and deliver my bombs, or go back home in disgrace. I rolled in.

To this day I still debate with myself whether or not I made the right choice. Life would probably be a whole lot easier for me today if I had not flown those next 288 combat missions. I had plenty of time to agonize over whether I made the right choice that first time.

This has been the most difficult experience to live with - the memory of having another human being in my gun sight and having to make the decision whether to pull the trigger or not.

My biblical education taught me; "Thou shalt not kill; "Love your enemies"; "Do good to them who hate you"; and "Pray for them who despitefully use you".

The feeling I experienced the first time I faced that decision and decided to pull the trigger has been forever etched in my brain. I was forever changed!

Now that I had a nothing job here in Coral Gables, and had to constantly watch over my shoulder for the

Thevis hit man, I began to feel guilty about all the people I had killed.

To make it worse, we had to fill out an after action report when we returned from each mission. The required information for the report was a BDA (Battle Damage Assessment).

This BDA included a KBA (Killed by Air) report. Before we could leave the action site we were required to get from either the Airborne FAC (Forward Air Controller) or the Ground FAC, a BDA and a KBA (Killed by Air).

Standing at the counter filling out our after action report we were frequently serenaded with the music of the season, i.e. Christmas, Easter etc. as we wrote on the report our KBA numbers. (This would become a very traumatic memory for me many, many, years later!)

For the first several months I kept a private log at 'home'; my 'Hooch"; the place where I slept (a plywood shack). When the total number of people I had killed (KBA) exceeded 1000, I couldn't sleep any more so I burned the log! At that point I had only been flying Combat missions for 5 months and had flown just over 100 missions.

By the time I left "Country" with 289 missions, that number had grown to more than 2000 people I had killed (KBA).

When I returned to the "World", the USA, I discovered that our Secretary of Defense, the Honorable Robert McNamara (a statistician by trade), had been accumulating all the reports from all our combat units of "Enemy soldiers killed that day". He then had the total numbers released to the press. Dan Rather had reported them every day on the nightly news.

I was somewhat relieved when it was reported that the total number of people reported killed on the nightly news, exceeded the total population of Vietnam.

Maybe the actual number I was responsible for killing as reported by the Forward Air Controllers were overstated. Even if it was only half of the number reported to me by the FAC's that meant I had actually killed more than one thousand people!

This knowledge became a huge burden. And I had been carrying it around for more than 18 years! Here I was in Coral Gables, waiting for the Mafia hit man to arrive and finish his job.

The EYEBALL

I started to Hallucinate. Ghosts in white sheets began to float over my bed.

The ghosts had Vietnamese faces and they would stare at me as they floated by. I lost so much sleep I couldn't function for days.

Then came "The Eyeball". One day I saw a movement up near the ceiling and looked up. There at the intersection of the wall and ceiling was an 'eyeball' staring down at me. It appeared to be about 2 feet wide and it never blinked. It also never went away. From that moment on, the eyeball was always up there. All I had to do to see it was – look up!

Then one day I got a phone call from my dad. Dad had retired several years before as an Officer at the Federal Correctional Institution in Tallahassee. During his 25 years at the prison, he had made friends with many other officers. Over the years, many of his friends had taken promotions and transfers to other federal prisons across the nation. After hearing about my phone call from the FBI telling me that Michael Thevis had put out a contract to have me killed, Dad started contacting his old friends at the Marion, Illinois Federal Prison where Thevis was confined. Dad was looking for help for me.

When I answered the phone, Dad said, "Rodney I just got a phone call from my friend in Marion, Ill." He said "Tell Rodney he can come home now. Tell him I just went down to that goddamn convict's cell and told that SOB that if anything happened to Rodney, he Michael Thevis would very likely have an accident right here in this prison. And I guaranteed him he would <u>Not Survive</u> that accident! Then I handed him a phone and recorded his conversation with his hit man. Thevis was so scared he not only told his hit man to cancel the contract; he added an offer to pay the man twice as much to follow Rodney around and make <u>sure</u> Rodney didn't accidently trip and fall and hurt himself!"

I thanked Dad for his help and hung up the phone.

I resigned my job and returned to Tallahassee. I told my wife I was going to the VA Hospital in Lake City and turn myself in for serious psychiatric treatment.

Without my income we would have to declare bankruptcy. I told my wife to just contact a bankruptcy attorney and let him make all the decisions. I was totally nonfunctional.

I got in my car and drove to Lake City, Florida and found the VA Hospital. At the hospital, I told them I was experiencing serious psychiatric problems and needed to be hospitalized immediately. I found out that they did not have an inpatient psychiatric facility there at the Lake City Hospital.

The doctor on duty asked me a few questions. When I told him about the "Eyeball", he asked me no more questions. I waited while they made calls to every VA hospital in the southeast.

Finally, they found one with inpatient facilities at Tuskegee, Alabama. The doctor on duty thought I should not be driving in my condition, so he assigned a staff member to drive me in a government vehicle, 350 miles to Tuskegee. We arrived at Tuskegee late; just before midnight. The hospital admitting office was closed. I was being admitted in the security office at the main gate. As I waited to be interviewed, a police officer arrived, escorting a somewhat inebriated young man. The individual was acting in a rather unruly manner. At one point, when the police officer was arguing with the young man, he backed up toward me and his holstered pistol was only inches from my face. Never before in my life had I ever had an urge to hurt myself, but in that moment I thought about grabbing his pistol and shooting myself in the head. The only thing that prevented me from doing it was knowing how much trouble that poor policeman would have been in, if I had. I just gritted my teeth and waited until the urge passed.

Later on this young man and I would become friends as we worked our way through the PTSD treatment process.

I was assigned a temporary bed that night and faced a barrage of interviews the next morning. Things were proceeding slowly until I mentioned "The Eyeball" as I had nicknamed the apparition I saw every time I looked up.

At that point the physician had me admitted immediately to the 'Lock Ward'. They didn't call it 'The Locked ward'. It was always the 'Lock Ward'. This was the ward where there was a perpetual suicide watch for all patients. I met patients with all kinds of mental conditions while I was confined in the "Lock Ward."

One day as I lay on my cot a young black man walked across the room and stopped at my cot looking down at me. Before I could say anything he said in a loud voice, 'White Devil'. Then he hit me with his fist as hard as he could right in the face!

Obviously he had been treated badly by some white man sometime in the past. Later on, he and I became friends; and I do believe that he had no memory of the 'White Devil' incident.

I was started on some very strong antidepressant medications and daily sessions with a psychiatrist.

About two weeks after I arrived, I was called to the front office. There was a man from the Social Security office. He told me that I might be eligible for Social Security Disability.

He asked lots of questions until I told him about the "Eyeball" always looking at me. At that point he seemed satisfied that I was really "Disabled" by my wartime experiences.

Shortly after this visit my wife started receiving monthly Social Security Disability payments.

Two things happened while I was confined in the hospital that has had lasting effects on my life. The first thing was getting rid of the "eyeball". It happened unexpectedly and quite by luck.

I had been to visit the dentist, and as I was leaving his office, I encountered the young fellow who was delivered to the hospital by the police the night I had been admitted. We chatted as we walked back to the ward about a lot of things. As we passed one building which I had not visited before, I asked him if he knew what was located in this building.

He told me it was the 'Group Counseling Building.' I was curious so I went in and asked if I could get into one of their sessions. The leader of the counseling sessions was a psychologist, not a psychiatrist like the doctor I had been seeing. I requested and got permission to attend a group counseling session.

If I had not seen what happened, I would never have believed it. This is what happened. Believe it or not – it really did happen!

We gathered in a circle of chairs. The leader of the group started by asking if anyone had something they would like to work on. No one spoke, so I asked him to explain what he was talking about – "Work On?"

He said, "Do you have something bothering you that you would like to change." I said "Well I have this large Eyeball, about two feet wide, which is always staring at me, every time I look up. Yes, I would like to get rid of it."

"OK", he said, "let's get busy!" The doctor put two chairs, facing each other, in the middle of a circle of chairs. The two chairs were about six feet apart. There were 15 combat veterans sitting in the circle of chairs.

The doctor asked me to sit in one of the two chairs in the center of the circle. I moved to the chair and sat down. Everyone became very quiet. After a few moments he said. "I want you to look at that empty chair and imagine that the person whose eye is watching you is sitting in that chair."

It got very quiet in the room as I tried to imagine a person sitting in an empty chair. Then the doctor spoke, "Do you have the person pictured?"

"Yes," I answered. The doctor said: "Ask that person why he is watching you."

I felt stupid, playing this crazy game, but I decided to go ahead anyway. I said to the empty chair "Why are you watching me?"

After a short pause, the doctor said "Change chairs!"

I really felt stupid, but I decide to keep playing his silly game and so I moved to the other chair. The room got very quiet.

In loud voice the doctor said "Answer the question!!"

I don't know where it came from, but a voice I have never heard before came out of my throat! It said:

"I'm watching you because you killed so many people in Vietnam you don't deserve to be alive."

At that moment I noticed for the first time that the eyeball was green, the same color as the eye I see in the mirror each morning when I shave. It was my eye! IT WAS ME! I WAS CONDEMNING MYSELF FOR KILLING SO MANY PEOPLE IN VIETNAM!

I started crying uncontrollably. The doctor had another staff member escort me back to the 'Lock Room.'

I have never seen that eyeball again. This happened in 1986 and I as I sit here in 2015 I remember it as if it were yesterday.

I later learned in therapy that there is a name for this treatment: it's called "The empty chair treatment".

There are so many PTSD symptoms like this that are never diagnosed by professionals because most veterans with PTSD, like me have never heard anyone tell them that THERE IS HELP! We are left to think that that we are just "crazy"!

After I returned from Combat I felt so uncomfortable being in close proximity to anyone I loved. My wife, my two beautiful daughters, my two wonderful sons, my parents, my three brothers and my sister were systematically alienated by my actions.

I had a compulsion to do things that would create space between us. I wanted to be close to all my loved ones. But at the same time I did not want any of them to be close to me. I know that it sounds crazy and I thought I was just hopelessly insane. I had not been able to find an explanation for these feelings for more than 30 years.

Then one day in a counseling session, I learned the truth. In all my missions in Vietnam I had not only shot at enemy soldiers; <u>they were also shooting at me</u>.

In my 289 missions I had looked down the barrels of too many blazing automatic weapons to number. At night I could see the tracers coming at me from every direction. They looked like little 'orange balls' as they screamed by my cockpit. They made a 'thud' when they hit my airplane!

My subconscious mind had concluded <u>that I was a target</u> and could expect incoming bullets at any time. Coming back home had not eliminated this subconscious expectation.

My subconscious mind had concluded that if any of my loved ones got close to me they would be in danger of getting shot! It was therefore imperative that I do everything possible to push them as far away from me as possible <u>for their safety</u>!

I wanted to be close to my loved ones. My subconscious mind wanted my loved ones to be far away from me. It was for their safety. I had been pushing my loved ones away for 18 years, not understanding why!

I was, however, very successful. All my family abandoned me except my younger son, Chuck, who has never given up on me. My wife finally divorced me and I didn't blame her. As I write this in 2015, my older son hasn't spoken to me for more than 25 years.

This, I believe, is why there are homeless veterans all over this country. They cannot understand why they are uncomfortable around their loved ones.

I also found out why we combat veterans have such difficulty talking about our experiences. We think that "No one can understand!"

The author of the book "Flag of our Fathers" never knew until after his father's death that his father was one of the men who raised the flag on Iwo Jima.

His father was like most combat veterans. We all say: "No one would understand"!

ECT

(Electroconvulsive Therapy)

Shock Treatments

The second significant event that occurred was "shock treatments" or as the medical professionals calls them "Electroconvulsive Therapy" (ECT).

The hospital had a wonderful medical library, and it was available to us the patients. I spent many hours studying all I could in order to understand what had happened to me, and what treatments were available to help me. One subject which really attracted my attention was the benefits available through ECT (Electroconvulsive therapy). When I asked my psychiatrist about it, he told me that they had used ECT with good results in the past, but the current hospital administrator did not understand ECT and was scared of the procedure. He had forced the doctors to stop using them!

I had been in the hospital for several months without any measurable improvement; so I petitioned the administrator to allow my doctor to use one treatment on me as an experiment.

After a month I finally got approval from the administrator to try it. I received three shock treatments in one week. For me, ECT was a miracle!

The treatment is a medical procedure in which the patient is administered anesthesia to induce a deep sleep;

then administered a muscle relaxer to prevent any flailing of limbs; and then a small current of electricity is passed from one temple to the other temple.

Each time I woke up after a treatment – I woke up into a 'different world'! Everything was brighter. Colors were more brilliant. I experienced a feeling of great anticipation. Something of great importance was about to happen. Gone was the feeling of dread that I had been carrying around for so long! I have always looked forward with great anticipation for my next Treatment.

Chapter 11

Return to Florida; Lose My Family
Find a New Life

With the combination of shock treatments, combat group counseling sessions, and individual sessions with the psychiatrist, I rapidly regained my self-confidence.

After five months of confinement, intense counseling, and receiving 10 shock treatments, I was informed that I could go home. By that time I had been a patient for five months; May until October, 1986.

I had arrived at Tuskegee by government auto. My vehicle was still in Lake City, FL, where I had left it when the VA provided a car and driver to transport me to the Tuskegee Alabama Psychiatric Hospital.

When I learned that I would be discharged, I called my wife and asked her to come and give me a ride home. I had been so sick and unresponsive for so long that we had lost all emotional contact a long time before. She had tried to maintain a relationship, but I had been emotionally incapable. We had not had much opportunity to communicate for the previous year and a half. She had driven to Tuskegee once during this time, but that was before I started my ECT (Shock Treatments). She found me totally unresponsive on that visit and did not come back again.

I never blamed her for not communicating with me then or during the year before that when I had worked in Coral Gables.

She was kind enough to come and give me a ride back to Monticello, but it was obvious that our marriage was over. Shortly after this, she moved into an apartment and we decided to get a divorce.

We met at the courthouse and found that we could get a divorce without a lawyer. All we had to do was fill out and file some paperwork and then wait a certain number of days until the divorce was final.

I never blamed her for leaving, and we were still able to talk. Although I did not have any bad feelings toward her, it was not an easy thing to accept.

She had been through a very tough time, trying to hold the family together all by herself without any help from me. The trial had been hard on her. Losing her salon business in Atlanta had been hard on her. Losing our mansion at the entrance to the Atlanta Country Club had been hard on her. Losing our 5200 square foot two story home with columns on the lake in Tallahassee had been hard on her. And now losing a mate was hard on her. She had just lost enough!

Chapter 12

The Wakulla Volcano

While I was in the VA Hospital in Tuskegee my Uncle Mike passed away.

After I returned home from the hospital, my younger brother, Larry came by to visit. I was living in the old house there in Monticello by myself. Larry and I talked of the many memories we had from our growing up years. Uncle Mike was a prominent figure for us in all of our memories.

Uncle Mike was colorful, boisterous, daring and brave. We reminisced about the wild stories we heard about his hunting and fishing exploits.

I never had an opportunity to hunt or fish with Uncle Mike, because he was still working during the years I was at home. Larry is eight years younger than I, so he knew Uncle Mike after Mike had retired. They camped, hunted and fished all up and down the Aucilla River.

The Aucilla is a very unusual river. In the space of 30

miles from the Gulf of Mexico north to Georgia, the river has 27 natural bridges. A natural bridge is a location where the river disappears down into a sinkhole and comes up some distance away in a spring, leaving a 'natural bridge' between the sinkhole and the spring.

Pioneer folks called these "Sinks", and "Rises". The last "Rise" on the Aucilla River, "Nutall Rise", is seven miles north of the mouth of the Aucilla River where it enters the Gulf of Mexico.

Between Nutall Rise and the gulf, the Aucilla River divides into two small streams for a distance of two miles, then the two streams rejoin and become the Aucilla River again for three miles before empting into the Gulf of Mexico. The island formed by the two streams is known as "Ward Island".

Larry had gone on many hunting and fishing trips with Uncle Mike after I joined the Marine Corps.

During our conversation, Larry paused; then said "You know, now that Uncle Mike is gone I guess it's alright if I tell you something he made me swear I would never tell anyone!"

He paused again and then continued "When Uncle

Mike and I were hunting on Ward Island, we weren't hunting for wild game; we were hunting for gold; pirate gold!"

I couldn't believe my ears. "Not Uncle Mike", I said. "He wouldn't play stupid games like that. Why would he be looking for pirate gold on Ward Island?"

Then Larry told me the story Uncle Mike had told him:

The Legend of Mandalay

When Uncle Mike was a boy he had a good friend his age who lived on a neighboring farm. This friend had told Uncle Mike many times about his family, the Parker family, and how they had come to Madison County. Then he told Uncle Mike the Legend of Mandalay. Mandalay is a community on the Aucilla River about a mile south of Ward Island. In the late 1800's, Mandalay was a destination site for sportsmen. Hunters and fishermen came from as far away as Gainesville and Tallahassee.

The area was remote. There were no major settlements anywhere nearby.

The Parker family had carved out a homestead for themselves in this rugged frontier, just west of Ward

Island. They had cleared enough land for a garden and built a comfortable home.

There was plenty of game and fish to compliment the vegetables from their garden. They were very happy in their wilderness home. The homestead was located several miles northwest of Mandalay and southwest of Nutall Rise. One evening as they were sitting on their front porch, an old man staggered out of the swamps, obviously lost and exhausted.

The family rushed to help him. He was carried into the house and made comfortable. They brought him food and hot drink. When he had rested he started talking.

He said he had been lost in the swamps for two days and had about given up hope when he found the Parker homestead. Then he told them the rest of the story about how he had become lost. Here is his story:

The Legend of Pirate Gold

"When I was a young man" he said "I lived in Tampa. At that time, 50 years ago, Tampa Bay was home port for many pirate ships.

One day, when we got old enough, my buddy and me

signed on as crew members on a pirate ship. We sailed the gulf from Key West to Mexico looking for ships to rob. When we had a good load of loot, we would return to Tampa and sell it to the dealers there.

On one trip we robbed a ship that had a big load of gold. On the way home the captain decided to bury the gold on an island rather than take it back to Tampa. He was afraid the other pirates at Tampa would steal the gold from us.

He picked my buddy and me to go with him to bury the gold. We were the youngest crewmembers on the ship, but we had heard stories about what happens to the men who go with the captain to bury the gold: They don't live to get back to the ship! That way the only person who knows where the gold is buried is the captain.

So, after we got to the island and before we buried the gold, we jumped the captain and killed him. Then we buried the gold and went back to the ship.

We told the crew that while we were burying the gold, a monster alligator came up out of the river, grabbed the captain and drug him into the water.

The last time we saw the captain, he was in the gator's

mouth and the gator was swimming up the river. The crew believed our story and no one wanted to go looking for the captain. We sailed back to Tampa and sold the loot. Then we sold the ship. After we divided the money we split up. My buddy and me settled in Tampa.

Every year since then, we have sailed back up here and got enough gold for another year. We've been doing this for 50 years.

This time, when we got close to the island, my buddy got real sick. He got hot, then he got cold. Then he got hot and cold at the same time and started talking crazy.

I knew that I had to get him back to Tampa in a hurry. I landed at the Island and went to dig up some gold for the next year.

When I came back with the gold, I found my buddy warming himself by a fire, but he had built the fire inside our boat! The boat had burned to the water line!

That night my buddy died. The next day I buried him. There I was in the middle of nowhere with no boat and no idea where I could find anyone in this swampland.

I started walking and I've been lost for two days. I thank you folks for your kindness."

Later that night the old pirate called the family to his bedside again. He told them, "I think I might be dying and I want you nice people to have this treasure map showing where the gold is buried."

He took the map out of his backpack and gave it to them, along with the $6,000 in gold coins which he had dug up to take back to Tampa for the next year.

The next morning they found the old pirate dead. They gave him a nice burial in the plot they had set aside for their family cemetery. Then they decided that the oldest Parker boy, a youth in his late teens, should take the map and go find the island and see if there was any more gold buried there.

The boy left with the map. He did not return. Three days later his body was found, floating down the Aucilla River at the Mandalay Campground. He had been shot in the back! The treasure map was nowhere to be found.

The only details the family could remember about the treasure map was that the gold was buried …On an Island, Up a River, Near a Volcano!"…

The Parker family was so distraught at the loss of their son that they decided to leave the wilderness and go looking for a more civilized place.

They packed up their wagon with all their belongings, including the 6,000 dollars in gold coins.

Then they headed north. When they got to Madison County they found rolling hills and fertile soil and decided to stay. They purchased a large tract of farmland and became very successful farmers.

A Parker grandson became Uncle Mike's best friend and had told him the story of Mandalay and pirate gold many times.

Uncle Mike believed the story and tried to solve the puzzle about where the "river" was, and where the "island" was, and how in the world did the "volcano" get into the story?

He finally decided that the "Island" had to be "Ward Island" and the "river" had to be the "Aucilla River" and the "volcano" had to be a figment of his friend's imagination.

My brother Larry continued his story: "For many years, Uncle Mike went hunting on Ward Island, but he wasn't hunting for wild game at all; he was hunting for buried pirate gold! He firmly believed the legend of

Mandalay to be a true story!"

After Larry left that day in 1986, I spent several days thinking about the "legend" and Uncle Mike. After spending five months in the Tuskegee Psychiatric Hospital it was nice to have something mysterious to ponder about to keep my mind off the "Invisible War" that was being fought inside my PTSD infested head.

As I pondered about the story, something just didn't fit. Uncle Mike was not a man to believe in fairy tales. He was a rugged individual, a no nonsense person. He had to have had some reason for believing the "legend" that was not apparent in the story I had just heard.

I sorted the facts over and over again in my mind, and finally decided that the "volcano" was the clue. If there had ever been any phenomenon in that area which could reasonably be nicknamed a "volcano" then there might be some truth in the "Legend of Mandalay".

I had lots of free time, so I went to Tallahassee, to the Museum of Florida History (the Gray Museum). Inside, I asked for the area where I could find early history of North Florida. I was directed to the second floor, South Wing.

I was really too embarrassed to admit that I was

looking for information about a volcano. I just started looking through the card catalogue and reading the index and chapter titles of books about the area.

I did discover a lot of tidbits about my home state that I had not known before even though I had grown up in Tallahassee. I was learning a lot but finding out nothing about a volcano.

After three days of searching, I was about ready to decide that "The Legend of Mandalay" was only a fairy tale.

Then, as I was about to leave the library one day, a young librarian came over to my table and asked "Can I help you find something?"

I was embarrassed, I but managed to stammer; "Probably not, unless you know something about a volcano over in Jefferson County."

She got a puzzled look on her face and replied, "No. I don't know anything about a volcano in Jefferson County." She paused and then continued; "but I have a lot of information about the Wakulla Volcano."

I almost swallowed my teeth! There were several seconds before I could speak.

I followed her over to her desk. She opened the middle drawer on the right side of her desk and lifted out a plain manila folder.

There was a simple label on the outside of the folder which said "Wakulla Volcano." She handed it to me and I went back to the table and sat down. I just stared at the closed folder for a long time before opening it.

Consider the ramifications. If there really had been a volcano, then there really could have been an island up a river near that volcano.

And, if there really had been an island up that river, near that volcano, then there could have been pirate gold buried on that island!

And if there really had been pirate gold buried on that island - it might still be there!

And if I could find where that volcano was located then I could find that island and that gold!

WOW! I might become rich and famous!

The Brown Manila Folder

I opened the manila folder with trembling fingers.

Inside were newspaper clippings with dates from the early 1800s to the late 1890's.

There were copies of pages from early books about life in North Florida which had been written in the 1850's and 1860's. I began to read, and I became more and more excited as I read. I just knew that I was about to become rich and famous!

This was such a welcome relief to have something to keep my mind off the Invisible War, and PTSD which had been wrecking my life for so long. The story started when Spanish Explorers arrived in 1513 at what is now the small community of St. Marks. In the ship's log, the ship captain had recorded what he described as a "volcano." He had observed smoke and fire in the swamps to the northeast of St Marks. The smoke could be seen in the day 15 miles out into the ocean. At night there was a pillar of fire that could be seen even further out.

For hundreds of years, Spanish ships had used this "volcano" as a virtual Lighthouse for navigating in and out of St. Marks.

In 1528 Cabeza de Vaca, a Spanish army captain landed with the appointed Spanish Governor of Florida and an army of soldiers 400 strong. They had come to claim Florida in the name of the King of Spain.

De Vaca kept a diary of their adventures which has been preserved and is now housed in the Royal Spanish Archives.

The conquering party landed somewhere near present day Sarasota. They were stranded after the landing by a hurricane which subsequently destroyed their ships.

They traveled on foot and horseback up the coast of Florida and passed the area near St. Marks.

In his diary, Cabeza de Vaca recorded seeing fire and smoke and described it as a volcano.

In the manila folder were also excerpts from newspaper articles and books describing stories which had been told to early settlers by friendly Indians.

These folklore stories described the Indian's beliefs about the volcano:

The first story was about a young Indian princess who was in love with a young brave. There was a dispute with the neighboring tribe and a war ensued.

The brave had to go to war, but the princess promised her Brave to build a large fire and stoke it with wood until he returned so that he would always know where she was.

According to the legend, the brave was killed in battle, but the princess is still over there in the swamps stoking that fire!

The next folklore story was about a tribe which lived near Apalachicola, and had been at war with the Wakulla tribe many years. They now wanted a truce.

The Apalachicola chief sent word that he wanted the Wakulla chief and a peace party to come to Apalachicola and smoke the peace pipe.

The Wakulla chief agreed and took a small group of braves with him to Apalachicola. Before they left, the Wakulla chief ordered his tribe to keep a big fire going with lots of smoke so he could always find his way home.

It turned out to be a trap; the chief and his party were all killed; but the Wakulla tribe is still over there in the swamps stoking that fire and making a lot of smoke!

Legends abounded guessing what the 'Wakulla Volcano' actually was. According to early pioneers, Wakulla is an Indian word. It means "smoke and fog (or mist)." Wakulla County got its name (Land of Smoke and Mist) from the volcano.

Anyone who has seen the fog banks roll into the county off the Gulf of Mexico, can imagine what it must have been like living in the area when the smoke from the volcano mixed with the thick fog coming in off the Gulf of Mexico.

Another article in the folder was about Princess Murat, the wife of Napoleon's nephew, Prince Murat. After her husband died she sold their plantation east of Tallahassee, and moved into Tallahassee. She lived on one of the tallest hills in Tallahassee, the "City of Seven Hills" She frequently entertained her guests by taking them up to a cupola on top of her home and showing them the "fireworks down in the swamps to the southeast."

The next item I found was a newspaper clipping from The New York Evening Post dated 1855. A reporter had visited Tallahassee and had experienced an evening as a guest of one local family.

After a sumptuous meal, the group walked to the capital building, went up into the dome, and watched the "fireworks" in the swamps to the southeast.

Local people believed it to be a volcano because it had been there since Spanish days.

The newspaper article was titled "The Florida Volcano." The reporter wrote that the phenomenon had the appearance of a "New Moon rising out of the swamps".

Every article and story in the folder spoke of the inaccessibility of the volcano. Many attempts were reported, but no one had ever gone into the swamp and returned to report the source of the fire and smoke.

This swamp had Cypress trees 3000 years old which were 16 feet in diameter and more than 150 feet tall.

Many of the trees had blown down in hurricanes over thousands of years. The result was an impassable mass of vegetation, as reported by Cabeza de Vaca.

One attempt to reach the volcano was made by a retired Judge White. The New York Evening Post had offered a reward of $10,000 to anyone who succeeded in reaching the volcano and coming back to report their findings.

Judge White took his party to St Marks and sailed his boat out into the Gulf. He then sailed east until he was due south of the volcano. Then he turned north and looked for a water passage to the volcano.

He reported that when he was headed due north,

toward the Volcano, he found himself in the Pinhook River. The river eventually narrowed and became impassable as it entered the Great Pinhook Swamp. He never reached the volcano.

Another article in the folder reported that in 1886 there had been an earthquake in Charleston, S. C. The quake was a 7.9 magnitude monster. It was reported by the National Geologic Survey to be so powerful that it was felt as far north as New Hampshire and as far south as Jamaica.

The quake shook St Augustine, FL with such force that it rang the bells in the old church tower.

In Tallahassee, several buildings were destroyed, and huge sinkholes were opened up in the bottom of Lake Jackson, Lake Lafayette, and Lake Miccosukee. All three lakes were drained dry.

<u>After the earth stopped shaking, the smoke and fire from the Wakulla Volcano were never seen again!</u>

At this point I stopped reading. I had found something that excited me beyond measure. The Pinhook River is 7 miles west of the Aucilla River. Judge White had reported that he was going directly north toward the volcano when he found himself sailing up the Pinhook River.

According to the legend, the gold had been buried "on an island, up a river, near a volcano."

Uncle Mike had spent his entire life looking on an island up the Aucilla River.

If there was an island up that Pinhook River, then that's where the gold had to have been buried. I just knew that I was about to become RICH and FAMOUS!

The librarian was kind enough to make copies of the key articles for me. I left the Gray Museum walking on air.

It was great to have something other than the Mafia and PTSD and that "Invisible War" in my head to think about. Early the next morning I went to the Jefferson County Property Appraiser's office. The Pinhook River is in Jefferson County, not in Wakulla County.

There I found an aerial photograph of the area which included the Pinhook River. Sure enough, **there about a mile up the river was a small island**.

I called my brother, Larry, and shared the news with him. We immediately started planning an expedition.

I wanted to tell everyone, and then I realized; <u>I</u>

<u>couldn't tell anyone!</u>

Two days later we launched our expedition. Our party consisted of two small fishing boats; the six of us, Larry's teenage son, Robert; my two teenage boys, Chuck and Rod, Jr., and Larry and me.

We found the island easily enough and beached the boats. After unloading the tools we started looking. Rod was the first to find something. His metal detector had gotten a hit on the beach near where we had landed our boats.

We all came running. After a frantic few minutes of digging we found the 'treasure'. It was a rusty old nail that resembled those I had seen in buildings in the old city of St Augustine. Wow! What an exciting find!

Again we split up and started looking. Then Rod shouted. He had another hit. We all came running and started digging. Another nail! We eventually found 12 nails in two rows roughly parallel. Then it hit me.

<u>This was the place where the old pirate's buddy had burned his boat!</u> These nails were all that was left of the boat.

We had found THE Island!!! Now we really got

excited! We just knew it for sure, we were about to become rich and famous!

We split up and started searching in earnest for that buried gold. After hours of looking and digging in all the likely spots, I found it!

In the center of the island was an old, old cedar tree. The tree had to be more than a hundred years old, and was surrounded by palmetto trees and undergrowth.

When I got through the undergrowth I found a small clearing directly under the Cedar. Then I saw it! A hole in the ground about 6 feet long and 4 feet wide which went down into the limestone.

Around the hole was a pile of loose limestone rock. This had to be the place where the gold had been buried those many years ago. Someone had gotten there before us.

It was probably someone from the hunting camp at Mandalay where the Parker boy's body had been found. The boy had probably asked someone in the camp for help finding the island. Whoever helped him, then must have shot him in the back and stolen his gold.

Darn! We weren't going to be rich and famous after

all. That was a somber trip back home. None of us said a word.

We didn't become rich and famous after all; but we had proven that a hundred year old legend wasn't a myth after all. <u>It was in fact a true story</u>!

And, we had discovered a piece of Florida history which had been lost for over a hundred years! There really had been a Florida volcano! The volcano had been named: "The Wakulla Volcano."

A month later I told this story at a meeting of the Jefferson County Historical Society there in Monticello. After the meeting an elderly lady came up and introduced herself.

She said "When I was a young girl, growing up in Gainesville, Florida, we were told a legend about gold! We were told that one of the prominent families of Gainesville had acquired their wealth when their grandfather returned from a hunting trip to Taylor County with an incredible amount of gold."

I was shocked when I heard this. I had not even mentioned Taylor County in my talk, but I knew that the east bank of the Aucilla River where Mandalay is located, is in Taylor County.

There had to be a connection. I searched for several years but never found anything in the literature about the Gainesville Legend.

Twenty years passed and then there was GOOGLE. I typed "Pirate Gold, Gainesville, Florida" and asked Google to search. Immediately there was the whole story. It was in the Gainesville newspaper and in the National Geographic magazine'

Emmett Baird had returned from a trip to the "Suwannee River", he claimed; and begun buying local businesses, paying for them with gold.

Baird told a story about meeting an old pirate on the banks of the Suwannee River near Fowler's Landing. The pirate allegedly told Baird where the gold was buried after Baird befriended him.

Wow! This was real proof that Uncle Mike's story of "The Legend of Mandalay" was not a legend at all. It was in fact a true story!

Many questions remain unanswered today about the Wakulla Volcano. What was the source of fuel for the fire and smoke which burned continuously for 373 years of recorded history?

From 1513 to 1886, and untold thousands or millions of years of unrecorded history before that, the smoke and fire had always been there.

In the manila folder there were varying attempts at explaining what caused the fire and smoke from the 'volcano'. Some speculated that it was a burning peat bog. But, with fire burning in the middle of an impenetrable swamp and the flames rising over 300 feet into the air, it doesn't seem plausible that it could have been from burning peat.

During the Civil War it was thought by the Yankees to be a Confederate salt factory and was bombarded by a Yankee ship anchored out in the Gulf of Mexico.

Before the Civil War it was thought to be coming from a camp of runaway slaves. None of the explanations have ever seemed plausible.

In March of 2008 I read in the newspaper where an accident had occurred in Oliver Springs, Tennessee. An oil drilling rig had penetrated an underground pool of natural gas. The gas was under great pressure from the depth of the pool and had blown the drilling rig completely away. A spark from the collapsing rig ignited the gas and resulted in a pillar of fire 300 feet high which had burned for weeks before the well could be capped. Smoke from the fire could be seen 30 miles away. The description of this disaster was almost exactly the description given by those early visitors to the Tallahassee area who wrote about the volcano.

The fact that it was an earthquake which stopped the fire and smoke from the volcano is further evidence that this probably was a natural "vent" from an underground pool of natural gas which provided the fuel under pressure to the surface.

The gas was under sufficient pressure to propel the fuel 300 feet into the air. One of the many lightning strikes in the previous thousands of years could have ignited the gas.

This theory of mine was further strengthened when it was reported recently that underground testing by a large oil & gas company had discovered a pool of Natural

Gas at 15,000 feet deep. The pool of natural gas reportedly extends from north of where the volcano was located to more than 100 miles into the Gulf of Mexico. The volcano would have been directly over the center of the northern end of this underground pool of natural gas. The "volcano" had been just been a pillar of burning "natural gas"!

Although I believe my theory to be correct, there may never be a scientific explanation for the phenomenon known as "The Wakulla Volcano."

This wonderful experience definitely contributed to restoring some of the joy of living and certainly provided a distraction from the "Invisible War" I had been living with for so long.

Chapter 13

Find a Job, Remarry

And

Move to the N. C Mountains

One day I read in the newspaper that the State of Florida was in the process of building a new prison in Jefferson County. They were accepting applications for some job openings.

I read the job requirements for the position of Business Manager and realized that I met all the requirements. I had earned three college degrees during my 21 years in the US Marine Corps, and my bachelor's degree from Florida State University was in Business Administration. I had 3 years' experience at Marine Corps Headquarters in Washington as head of Marine Aviation Studies and Analysis.

I applied and the job at the prison was mine. For the next three years I had a dream job. My areas of responsibility included Personnel, Accounting, Purchasing, Warehouse Management, and Laundry. I managed to find a staff of wonderfully qualified people. We were responsible for ordering all the building materials required to build the prison and maintain a complete warehouse of parts and supplies to repair and maintain all equipment.

Labor for this project came from a sister prison in Madison County, 25 miles away. The inmates were transported to our construction site in the morning and back to the Madison prison in the evening. Everyone on our construction project was terrific, well qualified and eager.

I took off two days a month and drove to Tuskegee for ECT (Shock Treatments).

Everything was wonderful! I was so happy I began to look for a mate. A friend introduced me to Martha. We began to see each other on a regular basis. I made her aware of all my medical and psychological problems. None of them seemed to bother her.

She introduced me to her children and we got along very well. I introduced her to my children, and they got along very well. I got acquainted with her younger son and his sons when I helped them build a six foot high board fence around their back yard. None of them had any construction experience and they genuinely appreciated my help. I really liked all of her children and her grandchildren, and they all appeared to like me as well.

Six months later Martha and I got married in Larry and Rosa's front yard with the Indian mound as a backdrop. My son Chuck was my only child to attend the wedding, but Martha's children were all there. Her ten year old granddaughter, Estelle, provided us with music playing her violin.

After the wedding Martha and I took off for Highlands, N.C. Where she had a mountain vacation cottage. I had never spent much time in the mountains, but I learned to love those mountains something fierce.

After that Martha and I took off for those mountains every time we could get away. On one trip we started looking at homes which were for sale, and talking about maybe moving to the mountains some day after we retired.

Martha was an elementary school teacher, but she really wanted to retire as soon as we could afford for her to quit. About a year after we got married she asked me if we could afford for her to retire right then. We were doing well with my job and my Marine Corps retirement income, and with her school teacher's retirement that should be all the income we would need. So I said "Go ahead and do it!"

Martha retired and immediately joined every garden club in Monticello and Tallahassee. I don't think I have ever seen anyone as happy as Martha was right then.

She had boundless energy and immediately started cleaning up the old 100 year old mansion where we were living. She came across all my Marine Corps uniforms which I had packed away when I retired many years before. She asked me if it was alright if she donated them to the theatre group at Florida State University to be used as costumes.

I had been very uncomfortable seeing those uniforms for many years because they caused me to "flashback" to that year I spent flying missions in Vietnam, and killing all those people. So, I said "Go ahead."

She did and I was amazed at how much relief I felt with all those war memories gone.

I loved my job at the prison; that is, I loved it until the prison construction was completed and prisoners were moved in along with prison guards. I found the prison guards difficult to work with, and impossible to please. They had worked with prisoners so long that that they had come to believe that everyone in the world was a crook.

While we were building our prison, the state prison system had automated all functions needed to operate a prison. Specialized computers were delivered to all prisons. When we received our computers and printers we delivered them to each office where they would be installed. It was my responsibility to supervise the installation.

My staff did a fantastic job until it came time to install the computer and printer in the Classification office. No one could find the printer which had been delivered to that office.

Our Superintendent assigned one of the prison guards the task of finding the missing printer. When he couldn't find it, he decided that I had taken it home with me (stolen it). He wanted to search my home! This was too much for me. I began to get some of my PTSD symptoms again, and started fighting that Invisible War all over again. I just resigned and quit. It wasn't worth it.

I went back to Tuskegee and checked myself in for another series of shock treatments. When I got back home I found that the missing printer had been found in the closet behind the desk where the computer had been installed.

The Superintendent wanted me to come back, but I didn't want to work around prison guards anymore, so I declined his offer.

Martha and I went to Highlands and started looking for a home. We found a property that needed some serious tender love and care. The property was a 4.5 acre lot on the side of a mountain with two homes; one normal size 3 bedroom home, and the other a smaller Guest House with 2 bedrooms.

The previous owner was a 90 year old lady who had lived there since she and her husband had built the houses 50 years before. Since her husband had passed away 15 years before, there had been no maintenance performed on the houses.

The neighborhood was a very upscale community with some homes in the adjacent community near the million dollar category.

I knew the situation with labor up on the mountain. The properties on the mountain were so expensive that none of the workers could afford to live up there. They all lived down in the valley and commuted up the mountain and back each day. Most of the contractors also lived down in the valley. Contractors therefore had to charge exorbitant prices for any work done on homes up in the mountains.

The children of this dear lady put the house up for sale after they priced the cost to have the homes restored. I made an offer so low I really felt bad about it, (about half the asking price), but it was all I could afford.

The realtor called and told me about their refusal and asked me what to do with my deposit check. I told her to just keep it with our offer and maybe the children would change their minds. A month later the realtor called and said "They accepted your offer!"

Martha and I were now the proud owners of three mountain homes. We put the old house in Monticello up for sale, and it sold right away. I gave my former wife half the profits from the sale and Martha and I moved to the mountains. I was back in the "Briar Patch" again, restoring an old house!

I knew that I must continue my shock treatments; so I went to the Durham, NC, VA Hospital (the nearest VA Hospital in North Carolina), to inquire about getting ECT treatments in Durham. The folks in the VA in Durham, N.C. welcomed me and immediately set up an appointment for a treatment.

I got my treatments every month, and really became fond of the doctor who administered them. I told him about my Marine Corps flying experience and about the time I had been an instructor at the Marine Corps Top Gun School for two years. The next time I went in for a treatment the Doctor presented me with a Top Gun cap. He had purchased it for me when he visited the Navy Top Gun School. This was such a meaningful gift that I still have it at home and frequently wear it when I attend FSU baseball games.

After about a year my Doctor was transferred to the Atlanta VA Hospital. On my next trip to Florida, I stopped by the Atlanta VA to say hello to my favorite doctor. He was enjoying his new job and introduced me to his new boss, a lady psychiatrist, Dr. Aida Saldivia. She was very nice and invited me to transfer from Durham to Atlanta to get my shock treatments.

I gladly accepted her offer as it cut my driving time in half. She made all the arrangements and I received a letter from her telling me when my first appointment was scheduled.

I received a shock treatment in the Atlanta VA Hospital every month for the next nine years. Altogether, I received a total of more than 150 ECT Electric Shock Treatments from 1986-2002. These ECT treatments were administered in The Tuskegee, AL VA, the Durham, NC VA, and the Atlanta, GA VA.

ECT certainly made life more pleasant for me, and probably saved my life on a number of occasions when I was stressed out almost beyond my ability to cope.

During the years I lived in the mountains, I drove 40 miles down to Greenville, S, C. once a month to visit the Veteran's Center to attend a group counseling session with other Combat Veterans. These sessions were helpful for me in living with the Invisible War, PTSD, which was constantly raging inside me. I found it easy to talk with other combat veterans because I believed they could understand the Invisible War I was living with since they too were living with their own Invisible War.

In one of these sessions, the Vet Center counselor suggested that it might be helpful for us to attend a "Welcome Home Parade" which was scheduled for Veteran's Day in nearby Hendersonville, N.C. I had never attended any patriotic event since returning from combat. I asked the other members of the group if any of them had ever attended any 'patriotic event" since returning from combat. Not one of them had ever attended such an event, nor had any one of them ever discussed the war with anyone who had not experienced combat. I decided to attend this one parade just to see if there were any combat veterans participating. I asked everyone in that parade whom I could speak to, if they had ever been in combat. I was not surprised to find that there was not one veteran in that parade who had ever seen a day of combat!

Chapter 14

Leave the Mountains
Move Back to Florida

After seven years in those heavenly mountains, Martha became homesick for her Garden Clubs, and her children.

We began making plans to sell the houses and move back to Florida. After I completed the restoration project for both the house and the guest cottage, we put them up for sale. The cottage sold first - to our neighbor next door. The main house sold shortly thereafter. We received 300% of our purchase price. Life was good!!

I had received a shock treatment at the Atlanta VA every month for six years. We moved back to Florida and purchased a home in Tallahassee. I continued traveling to Atlanta every month for my life saving shock treatment.

With the profits from the sale of our mountain homes we were able to buy a wonderful home in a very nice neighborhood in Tallahassee.

After buying the house, we had a substantial amount of money left for me to invest in the stock market. My years of experience as a stockbroker helped me establish a sizeable trading account. I continued returning to Atlanta each month for my ECT treatment. Life was good once again, very good.

With the extra money from the sale of our mountain homes and my stock market trading profits, we began to travel. Our first venture was to drive to Maine during December.

For some reason I was having trouble with the Christmas season and Easter season. It was the music that disturbed me. Martha had always been solicitous about my Invisible War, PTSD problems and was aware of my difficulty with Christmas and Easter.

It was against this background that we decided to take this trip to Maine so that we could be away from home at Christmas time.

As a retired Marine I had privileges to stay at military bases on a space available basis. We planned our trip so that we could stay at the nearest military facility on our route.

Everything worked out well and we discovered many things on our trip about our wonderful country. Everywhere we went we were welcomed by the military hospitality personnel.

We learned a lot about the defense capability of our armed forces. At one Naval base we checked into our room late at night and the next morning waked up, looked out the window and could not believe the sight!

Looking toward the ocean we saw a row of five submarines docked just outside our window. The view was breath taking.

After we arrived in Maine, I tried to find an old Marine buddy, Russ Treadwell. I had known Russ in flight school and later had flown with him for three years while we were in the Blacksheep Squadron in Hawaii.

It had been many years though since our paths had crossed. I thought there just might be a chance that he and Chris had gone home after he retired from the Marine Corps.

I knew that he was from Bangor, Maine and I tried to find him; but had no luck. Many years later, I googled his name and found that he had been the Governor of Maine! Wow! Knowing Russ though, I guess I shouldn't have been surprised.

We spent three wonderful weeks touring. We traveled from Florida through Washington, DC, and New York City, to Bangor, Maine and back to Florida.

We arrived back in Tallahassee just in time to celebrate the New Year 2002. Life was good, but that was about to change.

Shock Treatment Failure

The benefits from my monthly ECT Treatments in Atlanta were beginning to diminish. I no longer felt elated when I woke up after my treatment.

I was no longer anxious to return home and have some fun. I lost interest in Martha, my kids, my home, my world. I even lost interest in trading stocks!

On Thursday, before Easter I had my shock treatment in the morning and drove home from Atlanta in the afternoon. There was no elation when I woke up from the anesthesia, just pain and depression. I had just had enough. No more! I had no desire to remain on this planet any longer!

Chapter 15

Suicide Attempt

During the trip home from Atlanta, I planned my departure from the planet.

I knew that Martha and her sister, Betsy, would be going to Church the next day on Easter Sunday as I had heard them planning the event.

I decided that this would be THE DAY, Easter Sunday, 2002. I would depart the planet! After thirty three and one half years of living with PTSD (Post Traumatic Stress Disorder), I was tired, depressed, discouraged, disgusted, and possessed of a few other unmentionable emotions.

I didn't want to live with the guilt and memories of killing people anymore. I just wanted PEACE! I kept thinking of how peaceful death would be.

I spent all day Saturday getting ready. I cut the long hose off our vacuum cleaner. I then taped one end of the hose onto the exhaust pipe of my red Buick which was parked inside the garage. I used strong duct tape. The other end of the hose I placed into the back window of the car. I first lowered the window about 6 inches. Then I secured the hose in the opening and raised the window to clamp the hose securely. After that, I sealed the window opening around the hose with duct tape.

I was confident that there would be no exhaust fumes escaping the interior of that car. I didn't want any mistakes.

I wanted to get in that car the next morning, Easter Sunday, 2002, lock the garage doors; sit in the driver's seat; crank up the motor; go to sleep; and 'depart the planet'.

The next morning, Easter Sunday, after Martha and Betsy left for church; I sat down at the dining table and wrote a note to the family.

In the note I said: "Please Forgive Me! I forgive All of You! Love, Rod"

I then kneeled by the table and asked God to forgive me. I sincerely believed him when he said he would forgive everyone who asked. He knew I just couldn't take it anymore.

I then went into the garage, locked the door going back into the house, unplugged the garage door opener, started the car, and sat there smiling as the car filled with exhaust fumes. It was only seconds before I felt myself getting drowsy. I was so happy! No more pain. No more living through Easter and Christmas. No more fighting that Invisible War, PTSD. No more guilt because I had killed so many people. I asked God for forgiveness once again and fell into a deep, peaceful sleep. No more pain!! Death was so peaceful ...

<u>But that too was about to change!</u>

Chapter 16

Suicide Attempt Failure

Waking up Very, Very Mad!

My wife and her sister Betsy came home from church about two hours after I fell asleep. They couldn't get into the garage but heard the car motor running, so they called 911. Then Martha went across the street and asked our neighbor Bill for help. Bill broke open the door from the house into the garage, plugged in the power cord for the door opener, and let the fumes escape out the garage door opening.

The first thing I recall after waking up in the hospital was the awful taste of charcoal! I thought I had arrived in Hell – not in the place of forgiveness! Then I heard the voice of a human saying "Don't give him any more charcoal. I think we got everything out of his stomach."

Then the agony began. I realized that I had not escaped. Then the anger hit! How could I have failed?

What did I do wrong? Why did I have to stay on this rotten planet? It just wasn't fair! Why would God keep on punishing me? Why did I have to keep on living with this agony and guilt? ANGER, ANGER ANGER!

Then I began to upchuck the charcoal again. Ugh! What an awful taste! Anger, anger, anger! Why? Why? Why?

I spent a month in the Tallahassee Memorial Hospital, mental health ward. It was hard to accept the fact that I had failed. I had always succeeded at everything! It was so hard to have to admit that I had failed a dead serious suicide attempt!

After several days in the hospital, I met Dr. Alcera, a mental health psychiatric physician. She was from the Philippines and was preparing to retire from her practice in the U.S. and return to the Philippines. She was a very caring person and tried to help me as much as she could.

Like all the doctors I had seen in the past, she wanted to give me anti-depressants. When one didn't work she gave me a 'cocktail' of several anti-depressants. None of them helped at all.

Then she introduced me to an individual who literally did change my life. He taught me how to live with PTSD. That individual is Keith Ivey, a mental health counselor with whom Dr. Alcera had worked many years and trusted.

Keith is well known in the mental health community as one of the few counselors nationwide who were called to counsel the victims of the Oklahoma City bombing disaster.

Chapter 17

Living with PTSD

After being discharged I began to see Keith on a regular basis. He worked in a practice with a psychiatrist, Dr. Brodsky.

Dr. Brodsky stopped all the anti-depressants, and started me on a new medication, Neurontin (Gabapentin). The new medication helps me feel better, but the thing that has made all the difference has been the mental health counseling!

PTSD is not restricted to just combat experiences. I was surprised to find out that there are many events which can cause individuals to experience symptoms quite similar to combat related PTSD. In fact, there is a wealth of information in the psychiatric profession concerning effective treatments for those of us who are living with PTSD.

I discovered this when I met Keith Ivey. Keith first started me on a treatment known as EMDR (Eye Movement Desensitization and Reprocessing).

EMDR utilizes a memory recall technique familiar to almost everyone. It certainly was to me! The technique which enhances our ability to recall is the old, old method of looking up and to the right while trying to recall a specific event which occurred in the past. For example: 'Where did I leave my car keys?'

The therapist arranges two chairs so they face each other. I sat in one chair and faced Keith sitting in the other chair.

The immediate problem was my distress when I heard Christmas or Easter music. For years it had been necessary for me to leave town and take a long trip away from anywhere where this music was being played. The distress I experienced upon hearing any of this music was unbearable. I had no idea why I was like this. It was Easter Sunday that I had attempted suicide, and woke up very, very mad that I had failed!

After talking with Keith, seated facing him, about my distress with this seasonal music, he raised his left hand and asked me to follow his hand with my eyes.

He raised his left hand up and to the left. I followed his hand with my eyes without moving my head. This caused me to move my eyes up and to the right.

After about five repetitions, he said: "You are listening to Easter music." I kept watching his hand and moving my eyes up and to the right.

Then he said: "Where are you?"

Immediately, there popped into my head a memory as clear as if it was happening right then. The memory was of me standing at the debriefing counter in the hanger in Vietnam. I was writing my after action report. As I was reporting how many people I had just killed, Easter music was playing at a Church service close enough for me to hear it clearly.

I told Keith where I was. He kept moving his hand and I kept looking up and to the right.

Then he said "What are you doing?" Immediately I said "I'm writing a report about the bombing mission which I just completed."

"What part of this report is disturbing you?" he asked.

"I have just recorded the BDA (Battle Damage Assessment) which I received from the troops on the ground. They reported that I had killed 30 people with my bombs and guns."

At this point I started crying! After 34 years, I had finally found out why I could not hear Christmas or Easter music without experiencing extreme distress and trauma. It was guilt.

The exact same thing had happened at Christmas. Only then, I was reporting that I had killed 20 people while I was listening to the Christmas music.

I burned my log after recording that 1000 people had been killed by my bombs, but I hadn't burned the memory from my brain. It had been there, eating away at my soul for 34 years.

After I regained my composure and stopped crying, Keith said "We have one more step before we are through.

I want you to repeat these statements after me, <u>you don't have to believe them</u>, just watch my hand and repeat them."

Keith started his hand up and to the left and said: "Even though I have these thoughts and feelings, I am a good person."

It wasn't easy but I watched his hand as I looked up and to the right and said, "<u>Even though I have these thoughts and feelings, I am a good person</u>".

After several repetitions, Keith asked me to repeat the process, whether I believed it or not, using the phrase "<u>Even though I have these thoughts and feelings, I fully and completely love myself</u>." It wasn't easy because at that point I really did not love myself, but I did as he asked and said it.

I left the session feeling very different than I had before the session. I couldn't understand why I felt different, but I felt like I had just had a heavy load lifted off my shoulders!

I still have some difficulty with Christmas and Easter music, but it is not completely devastating as it had been for all those years. Now that I know why it was so devastating, it has been easier to live with the trauma.

Now I encourage everyone who is experiencing difficulty coping with life's stresses to seek help from the many mental health care facilities available in our society today.

I especially encourage all veterans returning from combat to seek counseling at the many Veterans Administration healthcare facilities available today.

Don't keep on like I did; constantly hurting and not knowing why.

As I write this, it has been thirteen years since that unsuccessful suicide attempt. During that time I have rebuilt my life with regular counseling sessions and substantial involvement in my community and my church.

Four years ago I lost my wife Martha who died after a massive stroke. We had been married for 20 years. She helped me through some very difficult years while I was searching desperately through this jungle called Post Traumatic Stress Disorder. Martha was a very brave and loyal supporter during all those years.

Yes I have Survived PTSD! I did not do it on my own. I've had a lot of help getting this far. Now I have a mission.

My mission is to reach as many combat veterans as I can and tell them that there is hope for them. They don't have to delay as long as I did before seeking help. I ask that all of you who read this book give a copy of the book to every combat veteran you know!

Please don't assume that veterans can get this information on their own. They can't. They are probably still lost in the same jungle where I was lost for those 34 years.

I am publishing this book myself and making it available for purchase on Amazon and other Book Retailers. I am doing this so that all who read this book will be able to afford to purchase a copy at the lowest prices I have been able to negotiate. I hope that each reader of this book will give one to every combat veteran they know. And don't forget the combat veterans who are living in homeless shelters, and those living in the woods.

One other thing that has helped me survive this long has been rediscovering my faith.

Before entering combat I had a very close relationship with Jesus Christ. I even thought at one time that I was destined to be a missionary.

After all the trauma of combat I lost that close relationship and even began to doubt the existence of God and Jesus.

During the trauma of the trial and the trauma of the Mafia hit contract hanging over me for so long, I lost a lot more of the close relationship I had previously experienced with my faith.

After waking up mad from the attempted suicide, I decided that God had left me here on Earth for a purpose. After that I reestablished a relationship with Jesus Christ.

Through this relationship, I have developed a trust in God that is stronger than I had ever experienced before. I now believe that everything I have experienced has been for a purpose. And I have discovered what that purpose is. That purpose is to share with the world what I discovered after I woke up in the hospital with the taste of charcoal in my mouth.

I discovered that Jesus loves me more than I ever realized before! I discovered that He has a mission for each one of us here on this planet.

And I discovered that He sometimes uses trials and trauma to prepare us for our mission here on this planet!

Epilogue

My new wife, Julie and I live in a Continuing Care Retirement Community, CCRC of just over 600 residents.

We love to be with so many people who are near our own age. We have so many activities available to us that we could never be able to participate in them all. We just select what we want and enjoy what we select. Life is wonderful!

Mob Boss Michael Thevis died of natural causes in a Federal Prison November 30, 2013 after serving 35 years. Peace at last for me! I no longer have to keep looking over my shoulder!

I see Keith on a monthly basis when things are going well, and more frequently when things get stressful. PTSD has not been eliminated, but it has become manageable.

I also regularly visit the Regional Veteran's Administration Hospital in Gainesville and our local VA

Clinic here in Tallahassee. The VA has always been there when I needed them!

This is an Invisible War we are fighting! You are not alone. Many others are fighting their Invisible War! THEY NEED YOUR HELP. Go to the Veterans Administration. They have hospitals and clinics; Vet Centers and people who know what you are living with. Give them a chance! See what they can do. DON'T KEEP FIGHTING THIS INVISIBLE WAR ALONE!

After you get help – go out and find others who need help and get them to the nearest VA Facility. Best of luck to you all!   Rod

Resources:

- PTSD and Veterans,

WWW. maketheconnection.net/PTSD U.S. Department of Veterans Affairs

- National Resource Directory

Crisis Resources – Veterans Crisis Line 1 800 – 273 – 8255 Military Crisis Line 1 800 – 273 – 8255,

National Call Center for Homeless Veterans 1-877 – 242 – 3838,

Veterans Administration Caregiver Support Line 1 – 855 – 260 – 3274,

Wounded Warrior Resource Center 1 – 800 – 342 – 9647

- National Center for PTSD
- National Institutes of Mental Health (NIMH)
- Therapy for PTSD

- National Suicide Prevention Lifeline – 1- 800 -273 – Talk (8255)

- American Foundation for Suicide Prevention. Center for Suicide Prevention

- Suicide.org

Suicide Prevention, Awareness and Support (national and international resources)

- 1- 800 Suicide (1 – 800 – 784 – 2433) Hotline – Treatment and Advocacy

- Crisis Center – International Association for Suicide Prevention (IASP)

- American Foundation for Suicide Prevention

- Links of Interest/American Association of Suicidology

- This is not an exhaustive list, there many other excellent resources, please add the ones you know to the list. In every community there are fine facilities, and skilled practitioners at every level of licensure and certification. If you have difficulty locating them reach out, to local VA clinics, Mental Health Centers, Certified Employee Assistance Professionals (CEAP'S), hospital discharge planners, Clinical Social Workers, Crisis Hotlines, and/or friends and family who are receiving services. You do not have to face these issues alone.

Made in the USA
Lexington, KY
05 September 2015